SpringerBriefs in Computer Science

Series Editors
Stan Zdonik
Peng Ning
Shashi Shekhar
Jonathan Katz
Xindong Wu
Lakhmi C. Jain
David Padua
Xuemin (Sherman) Shen
Borko Furht
V.S. Subrahmanian
Martial Hebert
Katsushi Ikeuchi
Bruno Siciliano
Sushil Jajodia

For further volumes:
http://www.springer.com/series/10028

Paulo Ferreira • Pedro Alves

Distributed Context-Aware Systems

Springer

Paulo Ferreira
INESC ID, Instituto
  Superior Técnico
Universidade de Lisboa
Lisboa, Portugal

Pedro Alves
INESC ID, Instituto
  Superior Técnico
Universidade de Lisboa
Lisboa, Portugal

ISSN 2191-5768   ISSN 2191-5776 (electronic)
ISBN 978-3-319-04881-9   ISBN 978-3-319-04882-6 (eBook)
DOI 10.1007/978-3-319-04882-6
Springer Cham Heidelberg New York Dordrecht London

Library of Congress Control Number: 2014936980

Printed on acid-free paper

Springer is part of Springer Science+Business Media (www.springer.com)

To our families

Preface

We have been watching a tremendous growth of available personal sensing devices embedded in smartphones which include multiple sensors such as GPS, WiFi/3G, accelerometer, and light sensor and can run a variety of applications. Thus, using such sensors, we can collect a large amount of context information such as location, time, user's activity, etc.

The availability of users' context information, given the widespread usage of such devices with several context capture techniques at our disposal, makes possible the development of distributed context-aware systems. These support new applications and services and may enrich user-applications interactions.

Most well-known context-aware applications (e.g., social software) operate on a large scale, i.e., they involve a large number of users generating and consuming a huge number of messages carrying context information (e.g., location). In such distributed context-aware systems, we face a scalability problem of a large number of producers (sensors) transmitting information to a large number of consumers (client applications) in highly dynamic environments, with different computing capabilities, user mobility, and privacy issues.

This book addresses the above mentioned issues: scalability and privacy in distributed context-aware systems. It is organized in five chapters starting with an introduction to the theme raising the most important challenges. Then, Chap. 2 presents several important definitions (establishing a common ground for the following chapters) and a taxonomy. These are important to Chap. 3 which describes some of the most relevant distributed context-aware systems that can be classified according to the taxonomy. Privacy is addressed in Chap. 4. The book ends with Chap. 5 that presents some important conclusions.

The audience for this book is wide; researchers, students, and professionals interested in the areas addressed may find most relevant information regarding scalability and privacy in distributed context-aware systems.

Lisboa, Portugal   Paulo Ferreira
Lisboa, Portugal   Pedro Alves
October, 2013

Acknowledgments

This book would not be possible without the contribution of the institutions hosting the authors: the research institute *Instituto de Engenharia de Sistemas e Computadores Investigação e Desenvolvimento em Lisboa* (INESC ID) and the engineering school *Instituto Superior Técnico* (IST). Both institutions have provided the authors with the research and teaching environment so much needed for a fruitful scientific and technological interaction among students at different levels (Ph.D. and M.Sc.) as well as among students and professors. We express our gratitude to both INESC ID and IST, to all the Ph.D. and M.Sc. students who, by their enthusiastic and hard work, have helped to pave the way for this work, and also to our colleagues in the Distributed Systems Group at INESC ID.

Above all we want to thank our families, who supported and encouraged us in spite of all the time this book took us away from them. It was a long and difficult journey for them.

Contents

Acronyms

AP	Access point
CPU	Central processing unit
CSCW	Computer-supported cooperative work
GPRS	General packet radio service
GPS	Global positioning system
GSM	Global system for mobile communications
GUI	Graphical user interface
HTTP	Hypertext transfer protocol
HTTPS	Hypertext transfer protocol secure
IM	Instant messaging
IP	Internet protocol
IR	Infrared
IRC	Internet relay chat
PC	Personal computer
RFID	Radio frequency identification
RMI	Remote method invocation
SIP	Session initiation protocol
SMS	Short message service
TCP	Transport control protocol
UDP	User datagram protocol
XMPP	Extensible messaging and presence protocol
WiFi	Wireless fidelity (IEEE 802.11b wireless networking)

Chapter 1
Introduction

Abstract In this chapter we start with a motivation for distributed context-aware systems. This is mainly related to the growing need for people to efficiently communicate with each other independently of specific tasks and location. Current widely used tools such as instant messaging and e-mail lack several characteristics of face-to-face communication often found on colocated teams. A promising approach is context-aware applications; these are able to adapt their operations to current context without explicit user intervention. Such applications raise the issue of context propagation which clearly poses several challenges regarding scalability and privacy. In this chapter we clarify such challenges and conclude by emphasizing the distinctive features of the survey in this book: basically, we describe the possible options that an application developer has to consider regarding distributed context-aware applications, instead of just enumerating the requirements.

1.1 Distributed Context-Aware Systems

Efficient communication and coordination among geographically dispersed teams is mostly done using traditional mechanisms such as instant messaging and e-mail. However, these are not enough to accomplish such communication and coordination efficiently. No one denies that these mechanisms and other forms of direct communication[1] have seen a tremendous evolution in the last years and are now essential for modern team collaboration; however, they still lack several characteristics of face-to-face communication often found on colocated teams. For example, it ought to be possible, for every team member, to become aware of what is going on: who belongs to the team, who is online, who is working on what, who is responsible for what, etc. [44]. This can be accomplished using direct

---

[1]Communication which is explicitly initiated by someone and whose recipient is known, be it an individual or a group.

communication where members continuously update their current status, but since it requires too much effort from them, it usually ends up being dismissed. However, dismissal of such information is not an option, as it has been proven multiple times to be essential to efficient knowledge sharing and learning [11, 34]. To better understand this impact, we can refer to Sawyer's work [84], who found that social processes such as informal coordination and ability to resolve intra-group conflicts accounted for 25 % of the variations on software development quality.

It should be clear now that direct communication needs to be complemented with other communication forms, but which forms are those? Which forms will allow us to propagate to all team members this indirect, almost surreptitious knowledge? Research conducted in the last decade suggests that the answer may lie in context-aware applications [85], which are able to adapt their operations to current context without explicit user intervention. This context can be defined by a multitude of variables such as location, time, or even emotional state. For example, a GPS-enabled device that is carried by every team member is sufficient to provide continuous location awareness without user effort (i.e., without the need of direct communication). With increasing availability and decreasing cost of this kind of devices, it is expected that context-aware applications become more common in many areas, including team collaboration. Still, these devices (also known as sensors) can only go so far in this process—although they are able to capture context, they do not know how to distribute it among interested parties.

For most context-aware applications, sensors provide information either for personal consumption (e.g., tourist virtual guides [25]) or for community anonymous data gathering for statistical purposes (e.g., traffic information or health habits [76]). In both cases, the propagation of context is simple, often using a direct channel between the sensor and the data consumer. However, propagating context among the members of a group is a much different (and harder) problem, because we are entering the realm of distributed systems protocols such as broadcasting and publish-subscribe. In fact, with these distributed context-aware systems, we face the classical scalability problem of N producers (sensors) transmitting information to M consumers (client applications) with some aggravating factors: highly dynamic environments, different computing capabilities, user mobility, and privacy issues [55]. Recent increased interest in social software applications [95] makes this challenge even more relevant.

Traditionally, distributed context-aware systems have been analyzed more from a usability perspective and not so much from the resource usage or scalability viewpoint, but we believe this is bound to change. The success of early experiments with small groups will necessarily lead to experiments with larger or more dispersed groups, using a much larger quantity of sensors. Nothing prevents massive sensor networks that are now mainly used for environment monitoring and disaster prevention to be deployed in multinational companies producing huge amounts of data, invaluable for learning and knowledge sharing. The underlying foundation is already in place: modern mobile phones (e.g., iPhone, Android smartphones) include a multitude of sensors ranging from accelerometers to proximity sensors (although still mostly ignored by the majority of the applications). A growing number of people maintain a virtual presence through most parts of the day, by logging in on their web-based e-mail account or just browsing and commenting information online (many times within their social network, a major source of context data), just to mention a few.

All this information must often travel across multiple networks and servers, until it reaches their recipients. A clear vision of what is going on "in the pipes" is needed to understand the surrounding issues for distributed context-aware systems. Only then, we are able to improve upon them and envision more efficient architectures and protocols for this kind of applications. This requires to specifically analyze distributed context-aware systems and their unique problems and challenges. Therefore, this book analyzes common principles of these systems and presents a taxonomy for comparing them.

1.2 Multi-scale Propagation

Context propagation may be needed or not depending on the application. Context-aware applications can operate on different scales depending on their purpose: personal, group, or community [55]. Whereby personal context-aware applications are designed for a single individual (e.g., personal finance), group applications are designed to propagate context among a group of people who share a common goal or concern (e.g., avoid interruptions when calling friends [72]). When attaining such goals is only possible with a large number of people, applications start operating at a community scale (e.g., traffic monitoring [43] or noise map of a city [73]).

This distinction is important because, as we move from personal to group and then to community applications, we have to face increasing problems related to scalability and privacy. In fact, it is undoubtedly much easier to propagate context to a dozen of friends than to thousands of strangers (obviously, at the individual level, this is not even a concern). For example, as of 2012, there are 175 million tweets (Twitter messages) being sent per day and some of these messages are distributed to over 19 million users (the number of followers of Lady Gaga).[2] Also, we are much more sensitive in revealing personal information to such large groups than we are to our close group of friends. For example, several people have been arrested or fired because of messages they posted on Facebook.[3]

Traditionally, application designers have decided to apply completely different mechanisms to the different scales. Firstly, community applications usually anonymize all information while group applications rely on trust between group members to prevent privacy breaches. Secondly, group applications propagate context in intact form while community applications aggregate context from multiple users into single statistical data. Thirdly, context propagation is immediate on group

---

[2]See http://bit.ly/zOiX8k.
[3]http://www.huffingtonpost.com/2011/08/30/arrested-over-facebook_n_942487.html.

Table 1.1 Differences
between group and
community applications

Group	Community
Members trust each other	All data is anonymized
Context intact	Context aggregated
Immediate propagation	Delayed propagation
User sees all context info	User sees only aggregated info

applications while community applications usually imply some propagation lag to prevent scalability problems. Finally, community applications usually present the information in a condensed form to avoid overwhelming the user with the sheer amount of captured information, while this is not a problem on group applications. These differences are summarized in Table 1.1.

However, we believe these boundaries will tend to blur in the future, as the distinction between personal, group, and community goals also starts to blur. As an example, consider the case of weight losing programs assisted by a context-aware application. Such applications track a user's weight on a daily basis as well as his diet, what he has eaten, how many times he went to the gym, etc. The main goal is clearly individual but it is a well-known fact that a group of overweight people can achieve better results if they work together.[4] On top of that, there is statistical relevant data from large communities that can help in the weight losing process, such as knowing that consuming a certain ingredient is usually related to weight losing from a statistical point of view. So, weight losing programs could benefit from the three scales but, since the mechanisms mentioned in the previous paragraph are usually applied to only one scale, application programmers usually end up choosing only one scale instead of embracing a *multi-scale* approach.

There are several other types of applications suffering from this problem. Typically, "friends location" applications are designed at group scale, but if they introduce features such as "popular places," they start operating at community scale. These applications are constantly propagating context between groups of friends (i.e., their location, current activity, etc.) to improve coordination between them, promote serendipitous encounters, etc. However, since they are already receiving this contextual information, they might as well discover the most popular spots (e.g., pubs, restaurants) based on the number of people located there (regardless of being friends).

1.3   Challenges

We are currently watching a radical change in the type of packets that travel on the Internet. Facebook and Twitter (among others) brought a huge increase in the number of personal short messages or posts, distributed in (soft) real time

---

[4]Take for example the TOPS (take off pounds sensibly) organization which is based on weekly support meetings between its (more than 200 thousand) members.

to a potentially large number of users. These messages are complemented with rich contextual information such as the identity, time, and location of the person sending the message (following the context model devised more than a decade ago [1] by the *computer-supported cooperative work* (CSCW) community). Context-aware applications were, until recently, created solely in the academic realm and were used by a handful of users. Nowadays, we have very popular applications like Foursquare[5] which has millions of users sharing their location on a regular basis, with more than 600 thousand updates per day.[6] We have traffic monitoring applications such as Waze[7] which relies on continuous updates with geolocation and accelerometer data from drivers' smartphones. We have real-time context-aware applications such as Highlight[8] which matches geolocation with social network data to provide "nearby friends" updates in real time. These are just some examples within the growing group of applications that use the Internet to propagate contextual information among a large number of users.

However, **context propagation creates unique challenges in the realm of distributed systems** [7] (in addition to their huge number): it is highly dynamic, it does not require user intervention, it has different levels of urgency, and it is privacy-sensitive. We now detail each of these challenges.

1.3.1 Highly Dynamic

To better understand how dynamic context can be, consider the case of capturing the geolocation of a moving person or the speed at which he is moving. To achieve a reasonable level of accuracy and precision, the system must capture and propagate this information very frequently, probably at least once per minute. Since these systems usually have hundreds of thousands or even millions of users, we are talking about a huge volume of information being sent to the server (assuming a centralized topology which is the case in the vast majority of the commercial applications on this area). Moreover, the server must then be able to propagate this context to whoever may be interested. The problem lies on the dynamics of those interests. For example, if the user is interested in receiving information about friends nearby, there will be a matching rule between his location and the location of his friends. However, if he's moving, and his friends are also moving, the system has to continuously change that matching rule.

For this reason (the dynamics of context), traditional publish-subscribe approaches are unfeasible since they assume a relatively fixed set of matching rules. On these systems, users subscribe to topics (subject-based systems) or predicates

---

[5]http://www.foursquare.com.
[6]http://blog.foursquare.com/post/607883149/foursquares-ups-and-downs.
[7]http://www.waze.com.
[8]http://highlig.ht/.

(content-based systems) [37]. Then, users feed content into the system (publish) and the system distributes events matching subscribers' interest with publisher content. Therefore, developing a "friends nearby" application using publish-subscribe requires each client to continuously change his interests. In fact, every time the user moves, the client application has to send three messages when just one should suffice: (i) publish the current location, (ii) unsubscribe from the previous location, and (iii) subscribe to the current location. This leads to wasted resources and poor scalability.

Application-level multicast tree approaches [18] fall on the same problem: they assume that distribution rules do not change very frequently. Although they still work on these conditions, the resources wasted by continuously rebuilding the multicast trees lead to poor scalability. For example, the Scribe system [17] relies on the following message types: JOIN, CREATE, LEAVE, and MULTICAST. It is easy to see the resemblance with publish-subscribe messages—changing the matching rules implies the propagation of a LEAVE message, a JOIN message, and a MULTICAST message (the latter alone should be enough to convey all the information we need, e.g., the new location, in the "friends nearby" application).

1.3.2 Does Not Require User Intervention

Context propagation does not usually require explicit user intervention—it happens in the background, thus increasing the usability and effectiveness of the application [7]. Thus, context-aware applications continuously monitor and propagate the user's context. Moreover, context information is transmitted unattended, i.e., without the user having to explicitly give that command [69]. Contrast that with the kind of traffic we are used to watch until recently. Be it an e-mail, a website, or an FTP session, the communication is always deliberately initiated by the user. This has been changing and the immediate consequence of unattended communication is that it will happen a lot more frequently. Humans can only send a small number of messages in a given period of time, but machines do not have these limits. In order to provide the best user experience, these applications will try to propagate context as much and as often as possible, since they do not have to rely on the user explicitly initiating the communication. This inevitably leads to a huge number of messages being sent to the server at a high rate, thus reducing the system's scalability.

1.3.3 Different Levels of Urgency

Finally, the urgency of context delivery is also highly dynamic. An application that enhances the mobile phone's contact list with the current availability of the others [72] must propagate context as soon as possible while an application that provides a noise map of the city [73] does not require immediate propagation (specially if it is not the city where the user is currently located). Even within the same application we can find different urgency levels. For example, CenceMe [59] captures user activity (e.g., dancing at a party with friends) and shares it in the social network. It makes sense to propagate those activities to close friends as fast as possible while acquaintances only receive those updates after a few hours. This behavior resembles traditional relaxed consistency systems [80] with the problematic difference of having some users requiring strong consistency while the others tolerate some temporary inconsistencies.

1.3.4 Privacy-Sensitive

The seamless integration of context-aware applications into their users' everyday life creates important privacy issues. People are sensitive about revealing their location or activities but these systems often transmit these and other types of context information without requiring a specific user action, in order to increase their usability. For example, the CenceMe system [59] transmits periodically the current user's location to a group of friends. It would not make sense to ask the user permission before each transmission and users are comfortable with automatic transmissions because they have previously defined with whom they are willing to share their location. In context-aware systems used by large communities, this may not be the case (again, the already mentioned *multi-scale* problem). Although previous research on this topic has mainly focused on the specific issues of location privacy (the ability to prevent other parties from learning one's current or past location [10,90]), privacy mechanisms for other types of context-aware applications are now becoming actively researched, propelled by the popularity of massive social network applications such as Facebook (for which people have already been fired or arrested[9]) or Twitter.

In summary, distributed context-aware applications have the potential to transmit a huge number of messages in a highly dynamic environment, therefore raising hard challenges regarding scalability. We argue that current approaches such as publish-subscribe [58, 87], multicast trees [18], or gossip-based protocols [4] are not adequate to these dynamics, because they assume the matching rules are fixed or change infrequently (therefore changes are too expensive). Also, since such classic approaches do not know how to extract semantic meaning from the exchanged messages, they cannot decide what is the most efficient way to distribute those messages—such a burden becomes the application programmer responsibility. Furthermore, although people are sensitive about exposing their context to others, context-aware applications usually do so without asking users' permission to increase their usability.

---

[9]http://www.huffingtonpost.com/2011/08/30/arrested-over-facebook_n_942487.html.

1.4   Other Surveys

Henricksen [45] includes a survey of middleware for context-aware systems. The article starts by describing common requirements for middleware in context-aware systems: *support for heterogeneity, support for mobility, scalability, support for privacy, traceability and control, tolerance for component failures,* and *ease of deployment and configuration.* The authors then analyze some middleware solutions (e.g., Context Toolkit [81], Context Fusion Networks [24]) with respect to the abovementioned requirements, but fail to provide a critical analysis of pros and cons of each solution. Also, these requirements are not design options but rather features that the middleware solution has already implemented or will implement in the future. For example, scalability is an obvious requirement for every distributed application, but what are the options to achieve it? The article lacks such analysis.

Bratskas [13] is similar to Henricksen's survey [45] as it focuses on certain *non-functional requirements* such as distribution, privacy, and fault tolerance, comparing several context-aware frameworks (not applications) regarding these requirements. However, it does not show neither the possible options for implementing each requirement, nor it explains why certain requirements are met and others are not.

Baldauf [7] starts with a layered model (Sensors, Raw Data Retrieval, Prepro-cessing, Storage/Management, and Application) to explain the challenges found on each layer on a typical context-aware system. For example, according to the authors, the *Processing* layer is responsible for (i) reasoning and interpreting contextual information; (ii) aggregating or composing different context data sources; and (iii) managing sensing conflicts that might occur when using multiple context data sources. It is also referred that this layer can be implemented directly in the application or in the context server and that the context server option may increase network performance and save limited client resources. It is also noteworthy that the *Storage/Management* layer provides two options for clients who want to access con-text: *synchronous* and *asynchronous.* In synchronous mode, the client is polling the server for changes while in asynchronous mode the client subscribes to the events it is interested in and on occurrence of these events it is notified by the server. The article also classifies the possible options for modeling context, that is, for defining how context data is represented in a machine processable form. These options are *Key-Value Models, Markup Scheme Models, Graphical Models, Object-Oriented Models, Logic-Based Models,* and *Ontology-Based Models.* Finally, it analyzes and compares the main context-aware frameworks with respect to architecture (how the different components are distributed), sensing (how sensor data is obtained), context model (how context data is represented), context processing (how higher-level data is inferred from raw sensor data), resource discovery (how components of the system are discovered, mainly sensors), historical context (if context can be stored for later analysis), and security and privacy (if it provides mechanisms for guaranteeing security and privacy of its users' data).

Contrary to other previous studies, in this book we describe the possible options for distributed context-aware application developers to choose on each layer instead of just enumerating the requirements. However, some of the compared dimensions are too abstract or mix different topics making it difficult to obtain relevant insights. For example, when comparing the architecture of the different systems, the authors of other surveys use the term *centralized middleware* as opposed to *blackboard model* or *widget based* (which can also be used in centralized middleware approaches). In fact, *blackboard model* pertains to how clients access the information and *widgets* are an abstraction on top of sensors—neither one is an architectural approach.

Chapter 2
Taxonomy

Abstract This chapter introduces some basic definitions related to context-aware systems and presents a taxonomy for such systems. Both are useful in the following sections. The taxonomy is well suited for guiding the architectural decisions of application developers; it is built around the four main layers found in context-aware systems considering context data from the moment it is acquired by sensors in raw format to the moment it is consumed by the end-user application: capture, infer, distribution, and consume. In this chapter we address each one of such layers.

2.1 Basic Definitions

This section introduces some basic definitions: context, context-aware systems, and distributed context-aware systems.

2.1.1 Context

The word "context" is subject to multiple interpretations and has been researched in various fields like psychology, philosophy, and computer science [12]. In the last field, specifically in the area of computer-supported collaborative work (CSCW), context was initially perceived as user location [14, 85] but, in the last years, it has been enriched with other sources of information such as identity, activity, and state of people, groups, and objects [81].

Still, the various definitions of context are usually synonyms of *environment* or *situation* which makes them difficult to apply in practice. In his seminal paper, Dey [1] came up with a definition of context that remains, to this date, one of the most accurate:

> Context is any information that can be used to characterize the situation of an entity. An entity is a person, place, or object that is considered relevant to the interaction between a user and an application, including the user and applications themselves.

P. Ferreira and P. Alves, *Distributed Context-Aware Systems*, SpringerBriefs in Computer Science, DOI 10.1007/978-3-319-04882-6_2, © The Author(s) 2014

By considering only the information that is relevant to the interaction between a user and an application, application developers can focus on a subset of the user environment data for a given application scenario. For example, the context needed by UbiqMuseum [15] to assist museum visitors is their location and native language. Other environmental information such as their body temperature or their marital status is not relevant to the interaction with UbiqMuseum.

Satyanarayanan [83] refers to context in its relation with pervasive systems that, with minimal intrusion, must be cognizant of its user's state and surroundings and must modify its behavior based on this information. A user's context can be quite rich, consisting of attributes such as physical location, physiological state (such as body temperature and heart rate), emotional state (such as angry, distraught, or calm), personal history, daily behavioral patterns, and so on.

Chen [22], not satisfied by a general definition, defines context by enumerating examples of contexts:

- computing context, such as network connectivity, communication costs, and communication bandwidth, and nearby resources such as printers, displays, and workstations;
- user context, such as the user's profile, location, people nearby, even the current social situation;
- physical context, such as lighting, noise levels, traffic conditions, and temperature;
- time context, such as time of a day, week, month, and season of the year.

These types of context are further refined by Dey [1]. He considers that there are certain types of context that are, in practice, more important than others for characterizing the situation of a particular entity: *location*, *identity*, *activity*, and *time*. These context types not only answer the questions of who, what, when, and where but also act as identity indexes into other sources of contextual information. For example, given a person's identity, we can acquire many pieces of related information such as phone numbers, addresses, e-mail addresses, birth date, list of friends, relationships to other people in the environment, etc. With an entity's location, we can determine what other objects or people are near the entity and what activity is occurring near the entity. This characterization helps designers to choose which context to use in their applications, structure the context they use, and search out other relevant context.

2.1.2 Context-Aware Systems

Given the characterization of *context* in the previous section, we now describe how systems use that *context*.

Schilit [85] defined context-aware systems as systems that *adapt* themselves to context. He claims that it is not enough to be informed about context. However, some authors say otherwise [64]. In fact, there is a classical debate in this area between

Fig. 2.1 Typical
context-aware architecture

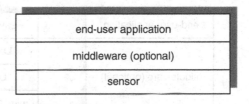

"use context" advocates and "adapt to context" advocates. Although research has been more active on systems that adapt to context, even an application that simply displays the context of user's environment can be considered context-aware, even though it is not modifying its behavior.

Dey [1] tried to conciliate both views with the following definition:

A system is context-aware if it uses context to provide relevant information and/or services to the user, where relevancy depends on the user's task.

In practice, this definition results in three main features that context-aware systems may provide:

- *presentation* **of information and services to a user**—systems that provide information to the user augmented with contextual information (e.g., phone's contact list enhanced with location information) or that provide services based on the current user's context (e.g., show me restaurants nearby);
- **automatic** *execution* **of a service**—systems that execute a service automatically based on the current context (e.g., automatically updating my status on a social network based on accelerometer data—sleeping, walking, and running);
- *tagging* **of context to information for later retrieval**—systems that are able to associate digital data with the user's context (e.g., virtual notes that are attached to certain locations, for others to see).

It is noteworthy that a context-aware application does not actually determine why a situation is occurring, but the designer of the application does. The designer uses incoming context to determine why a situation is occurring and uses this to encode some action in the application.

2.1.3 Distributed Context-Aware Systems

Distributed context-aware systems can be described as *end-user applications* that use context information provided by *sensors*. From an architectural point of view, these two layers (sensors and end-user applications) are mandatory, as they are the producers and consumers of context information. Between them, there is often a *middleware* layer to address communication and coordination issues between distributed components [45] (see Fig. 2.1).

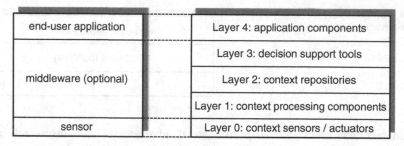

Fig. 2.2 Layers of a context-aware application according to Henricksen

In simple context-aware systems, the end-user application communicates directly with the sensor (e.g., a mobile phone that automatically switches off GPS when battery is below a certain capacity), removing the need for an intermediate layer. This was the case in early systems which were no more than distributed application components communicating directly with local or remote sensors. Today, it is widely acknowledged that additional infrastructural components are desirable, in order to reduce the complexity of distributed context-aware applications, improve maintainability, and promote reuse. Henricksen [45] enumerates the following five layers, as shown in Fig. 2.2 (relation to previous figure layers also indicated):

- context sensors and actuators that provide the interface with the environment, either by capturing it (sensors) or by modifying it (actuators) (layer 0);
- components that (i) assist with processing sensor outputs to produce context information that can be used by applications and (ii) map update operations on the higher-order information back down to actions on actuators (layer 1);
- context repositories that provide persistent storage of context information and advanced query facilities (layer 2);
- decision support tools that help applications to select appropriate actions and adaptations based on the available context information (layer 3);
- application components that are integrated in client applications using programming toolkits (layer 4).

Context-aware systems can be categorized into two large groups: local and distributed (see Fig. 2.3). Local systems are systems in which sensors and applications are tightly coupled (usually through a direct physical connection). For example, a mobile phone application that sets the mode to silent, while its owner is jogging, is a local system, since the accelerometer that provides the "running" context is directly attached to the mobile phone as well as the application that uses that context to activate the silent mode.

On the other hand, distributed context-aware systems do not have a direct physical connection between the sensor and the application. As a consequence of that loose coupling, it is possible to have multiple applications receiving information from the same sensor. Also, it is possible that multiple dispersed sensors produce information to be consumed by a single application. For example, a mobile phone

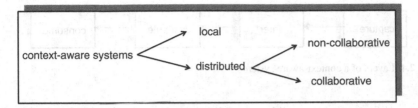

Fig. 2.3 Types of context-aware systems

may broadcast to a group of friends that its owner is currently walking, to decrease the probability of incoming calls during that period. In this case, the accelerometer is not tightly coupled to the recipient of its information.

We can further divide distributed context-aware systems into two types: collaborative and non-collaborative. Distributed collaborative systems are systems that help two or more dispersed humans accomplish a common goal. For example, MyVinc [40] provides real-time availability information within a group of colleagues, using speech detection, location, computer activity, and calendar entries. In this case, the common goal is team synchronization (actually, team synchronization is the most common goal of distributed collaborative systems). In contrast, non-collaborative systems support only individual goals. For example, UbiqMuseum [15] provides context-aware information to museum visitors. A portable device is provided to the visitors that, based on their current location and individual profile, shows relevant information in their preferred language. In this system, the goal is individual (the device shows information that is only relevant to its user) but the system is distributed since the location is inferred from Bluetooth emitters carefully dispersed throughout the museum.

2.2 Taxonomy Rationale

As explained in Sect. 1.4, existing taxonomies for distributed context-aware systems are not well suited for guiding the architectural decisions of application developers. We believe the main challenge of developing these systems is related to how the different layers communicate with each other and, mainly, how to overcome the problems that arise when these layers are spread across a distributed system. Thereby, we propose a taxonomy that:

- clearly categorizes the architectural options available to the application developer, explaining the advantages and disadvantages of each approach;
- analyzes the problems that are specific to distributed context-aware systems, whose (distributed) components have to communicate with each other, and how that affects availability and scalability of such systems;

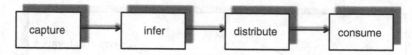

Fig. 2.4 Layers of a context-aware system

- exemplifies each option with real applications that were deployed and evaluated by end users, instead of relying on generic toolkits, frameworks, and prototypes.

To develop this taxonomy, we divide the analysis into four layers that we can find in the majority of these systems. These layers are traversed by context data, from the moment it is acquired from sensors in raw format to the moment it is consumed by the end-user application, as we can see in Fig. 2.4.

First, context data is **captured** from the environment using sensors. This data is usually too detailed to be used directly by end-user applications, so a **context-inference step** is needed to obtain higher-level aggregated data. For example, a GPS device captures geographical coordinates from which a place (city, building, etc.) is inferred. This step is also known as *feature extraction*. As the name implies, distributed context-aware systems have to deal with **distribution of context data** among its components in an efficient and scalable manner. Finally, client applications **consume** this information in order to provide relevant services to their users. Note that we intentionally left out the often referred in literature *storage layer* because, in this study, we want to focus on how context data is propagated. We now describe in more detail the available options to choose from in each of these layers.

2.3 Capture

The Capture layer is responsible for acquiring context data from the environment using sensors. Note that the word "sensor" not only refers to sensing hardware but also to every data source which may provide usable context information [7]. Sensors have been traditionally classified in two dimensions that, although differently named, are very similar. Prekop [66] calls these dimensions *external* and *internal* and Hofer [47] refers to *physical* and *logical*. We adopt the names proposed by Indulska [49], *physical* and *virtual* sensors, as depicted in Fig. 2.5.

Physical sensors are hardware sensors capable of capturing physical data such as light, audio, motion, and location. Location is, by far, the most researched type of physical sensor with numerous published studies from which we highlight the work of Hightower [46] and Indulska [49]. The latter presents the following taxonomy:

- **Proximity vs. position**—Position sensors provide the location of an entity with coordinates (e.g., the latitude and longitude of a GPS system), while proximity

Fig. 2.5 Capture layer

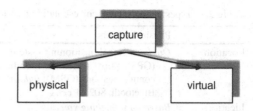

sensors provide the location within a region (e.g., mobile phone cells). Note that both modes have different accuracy levels, ranging from centimeters to tens of meters.

- **Line of sight**—Some location sensors require a clear line of sight between them and the associated infrastructure. For example, GPS sensors need a clear line of sight to multiple satellites, which prevents these devices from being used inside buildings. Systems built upon communication mechanisms that can cross clothes and walls place fewer constraints on device and infrastructure placement, but may not be appropriate when walls are, in fact, an important aid to infer the location (e.g., the room a certain person is in). This is similar to the distinction made by Chen [22] on "outdoors vs. indoors vs. hybrid systems."
- **Complexity trade-off**—Typically, location devices work coupled to an infrastructure (e.g., GPS devices and satellites), and their complexity is inversely proportional to the infrastructure's complexity. For example, a GPS device can be considered a simple device (if we consider only the receiver) but needs a complex satellite infrastructure. On the other hand, a location system based on multiple uncoordinated base stations or beacons like Cricket [68] has a simpler infrastructure but the device has now the responsibility of computing the position.
- **Identification**—Many sensor devices incorporate some unique ID that must be transmitted to the associate infrastructure to infer their location (e.g., WiFi), raising privacy and ethical issues. Sensors that compute the location on the device itself (e.g., Cricket [68]) allow greater end-user control over publishing their location in the system.

Virtual sensors acquire context data from software applications, operating systems, and networks [49]. Detecting new appointments on an electronic calendar and watching the file system for changes are examples of virtual sensors. These sensors can also be used to infer *location*. Indulska [49] gives some examples such as using a travel-booking system or the IP address of the active device[1] to perceive where the user is currently located. Although virtual sensors have not been subject to the same level of research of their physical counterparts, they offer a promising alternative as people spend increasing time using computers, smartphones, and similar devices, where their identity, location, and activity may be tracked easily with simple software. Actually, it is usually cheaper to develop and deploy a virtual sensor than a physical one, since the required infrastructure is already in place.

---

[1]The device where user's activity was last detected.

Table 2.1 Types of context and corresponding physical and virtual sensor

	Physical sensors	Virtual sensors
Location	*Outdoor*: global positioning system (GPS), global system for mobile communications (GSM); *indoor*: Bluetooth, 802.11 cells	Networked calendar system, travel-booking system, user's login on location-aware computer, IP subnet
Identity	*Based on something you are*: fingerprint reader, retina scanner, microphone; *based on something you have*: smart card reader, RFId	Various authentication schemes at the operating system or application level
Activity	Mercury switch, accelerometer, motion detector, thermometer, UV sensors, camera	Keyboard or mouse activity, application usage
Time	Clock	Operating system timer

The literature also refers to a third type of sensor, the *logical sensor*, which combines physical or virtual sensing data with information from other sources (e.g., databases) in order to produce higher-level context data [7,49]. We think the distinction between logical sensors and context inference is not very clear and prefer to include in this layer only sensors that capture information in raw format, without further processing. Indulska [49] argues that a distinction is made between logical sensors and the fusion of sensor data. According to him, logical sensors work with data from particular sensor systems and do not try to resolve conflicts. We still think this is a weak distinction because since, by definition, logical sensors gather data from multiple sources, it is impossible to guarantee that there will not be any sensing conflicts.

Different sensors can provide different types of context. According to Dey [1], the most important types of context are *location*, *identity*, *activity*, and *time*, corresponding roughly to the primal questions *where*, *who*, *what*, and *when*. When designing a context-aware system, it is important to know which types of context the application will want to observe and use the appropriate sensors. In Table 2.1 we show examples of physical and virtual sensors grouped by the type of context they are able to capture.

In Table 2.2, we show some context-aware applications and their corresponding sensors. Table 2.2 reflects a general trend in context-aware applications: while early applications were predominantly based on location sensors, researchers have been recently using other types of sensors to infer richer context information such as user activities (walking, running) and even mood (sad, happy) [82].

2.4 Infer

The *Context-Inference* layer, also known as the Preprocessing layer [7], is responsible for reasoning and interpreting raw context information provided by sensors on the Capture Layer. Most of the times, sensorial information is too fine grained,

Table 2.2 Some context-aware applications and corresponding sensors

	Description	Sensors used
GUIDE [25]	Information for city visitors	WiFi (location)
Welbourne [97]	Mode of transit: walking, running, riding a vehicle	Clock, GSM/WiFi (location), accelerometer
ContextContacts [62]	Enhanced phone's contact list	GSM, phone activity, Bluetooth (nearby environment)
UbiqMuseum [15]	Assists museum visitors	Bluetooth (location)
AwareMedia [9]	Support coordination at an operation ward	Bluetooth (location), video camera, shared calendar
Stiefmeier [91]	Help workers perform critical and complex assembly tasks in a car production environment	Body-worn, car-mounted, and tool-mounted accelerometers
BikeNet [36]	Cyclist experience mapping	Magnetometer, inclinometer, speedometer, microphone, GPS, GSR stress monitor, CO^2 meter
CenceMe [59]	Social activities (dancing, lunching)	Microphone, GPS, camera, Bluetooth (nearby environment), accelerometer
SoundSense [57]	Music events' sharing	Microphone, camera, GPS
Upcase [82]	Daily activities (working, driving, sleeping, resting, walking outside)	Luminosity, microphone, temperature, accelerometer

with too much detail for the needs of end-user applications. A classical example is location information provided by GPS devices. Generally, end-user applications do not need to know the exact latitude and longitude of an entity, being much more interested in knowing the place (city, street, etc.) in which the entity is located. A transformation is needed to reach a higher level of abstraction like transforming GPS coordinates into the name of a street. This transformation is commonly known as context inference, because it usually involves some kind of reasoning. Some authors [86] introduce a sub-layer called *feature extraction*. *Feature extraction* refers to the act of cataloging raw sensorial data into relevant features (e.g., from the readings of a luminosity sensor extract level, flickering, wavelength, etc.). Further inference can be made using these features. Zander [100] uses the term "context provider" as something that converts any kind of input data (either sensorial or web-based content) to an RDF-based context description.

Also, this layer is normally associated with classification techniques, mostly borrowed from Artificial Intelligence (AI) algorithms, such as Kohonen self-organizing maps (KSOMs) [54], k-nearest neighbor [94], and neural networks [74]. These techniques have been successfully applied to some context domains such as inferring the user activity (walking, running) from an accelerometer [97].

Fig. 2.6 Infer layer

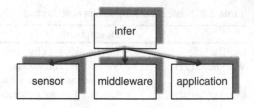

Context-inference techniques is an active topic of research which we do not detail in this book. Since we are analyzing *distributed* context-aware systems, we classify these systems based on *where* the inference occurs.

Usually, the type of information inferred from sensorial data is specific to each application. For example, consider the data provided by an accelerometer. An application might use that information to know whether a user is walking or running [97], while another may be more interested in detecting screw tightening [91]. In these cases, it makes sense to move the inferring task to the application because of the specific semantic needs it tries to accomplish. However, transforming raw sensorial data into high-level context information can be a resource-demanding task, unsuitable for applications that run on constrained devices like mobile phones. To avoid this problem, some systems use a middleware component (e.g., Solar [23], PACE [45]), running in a machine with higher capability that is responsible for context inference. In these systems, the processing is moved off the applications into a server, allowing the use of very basic devices for client applications. In other systems, the sensors are capable of inferring high-level context data themselves. For example, the Activity widget provided by the Context Toolkit [81] senses the current activity level at a location such as a room, using a microphone. Instead of producing raw audio data captured by the microphone, it provides a high-level attribute "Activity Level" with three possible values: *none*, *some*, or *a lot*.

In summary, context may be inferred in the sensor, in a middleware component, or in the end-user application. These three locations, depicted in Fig. 2.6, are intimately related to the following properties of a context-aware system:

- **Network bandwidth consumption**—Since context inference transforms fine-grained sensorial information into coarse-grained high-level data, it effectively reduces the amount of information needed to represent a context message. Thus, moving the inference layer closer to the sensor results in less network bandwidth consumption. This is more significant in distributed context-aware systems with devices dispersed along a wide area network, unreliable or low-bandwidth connections, etc.
- **Complexity (CPU/memory consumption)**—As already noted, context-inference mechanisms can lead to high CPU and RAM consumption, specially when sophisticated AI algorithms like neural networks [99] or decision trees [71] are used. Even if the device is capable of computing the information, it can lead to excessive and unsustainable battery consumption. Since resource-constrained devices are, in these cases, unsuitable for context inference, the developer has

to deploy the inference engine in a resourceful machine (e.g., a server). Most physical sensors are attached to low-capability devices (to increase mobility) and do not provide context-inference mechanisms. However, virtual sensors often run on servers or desktop computers (where they can access virtual context information from databases, shared calendars, etc.), so they are able to provide higher-level context information than their physical counterparts.

- **Reusability**—Context-inference reusability makes sense for context types as location, where the output is sufficiently *standard* to be used by multiple applications. For example, inferring the street name from geographical GPS coordinates is a recurring requirement in location-aware systems and does not make sense to (re)implement in every end-user application. Similarly to network bandwidth, moving the inference layer closer to the sensor increases reusability. In fact, reusability is referred as one of the main benefits of Context Toolkit Widgets [81].

- **Personalization**—Somehow opposed to reusability is the ability to personalize the inference engine to better suit individual needs. For example, CenceMe [59] is a phone application that allows its users to associate a certain movement (like drawing an imaginary circle with the phone) to some meaning or activity (e.g., going to lunch). Although it is possible to personalize a context engine outside the application, such system would suffer from scalability issues trying to cope with the individual needs of its users. Another important issue related to personalization is the mediation of ambiguity [33]. Sometimes, context inference includes dealing with ambiguous data and explicit user mediation is needed (the application prompts the user to resolve ambiguity) [39], again adapting the inference mechanism to suit individual needs.

Figure 2.7 summarizes how these properties are affected by the location of the context-inference engine. Moving the context inference from the sensor to the application achieves better personalization but higher network bandwidth consumption and decreased reusability. The most complex inference engines should be moved into the middleware where they have access to better hardware resources.

Some systems use a hybrid approach where the inference engine resides in multiple places. Miluzzo [59] proposes a split-level classification for its CenceMe system, pushing some classification to the phone and other to the back-end servers (middleware). The phone's classification output is sent to the server which then applies a second more complex classification. This design achieves a good balance between network bandwidth consumption (which is reduced because the phone sends already classified information instead of raw data) and CPU/memory consumption (complex classification is moved off of the phone).

Chen [23], in the Solar system, proposes an interesting solution to achieve personalization without sacrificing reusability. Applications can push its application-specific processing into the network as a proxy. These proxies run on servers in the network and form an *operator graph*, where multiple sensors can feed the proxies which can be combined with other proxies and reused by multiple

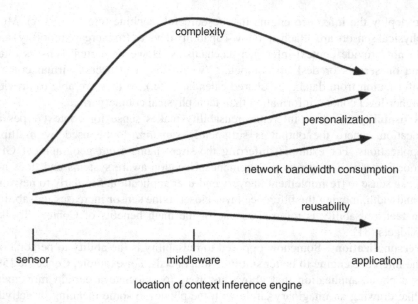

Fig. 2.7 How context-aware systems properties are affected by the location of the context-inference engine

applications, as shown in Fig. 2.8. The Solar middleware is, in fact, composed of multiple application-specific inference engines developed in a modular way such that multiple applications can combine and reuse them to satisfy their requirements.

2.5 Distribution

Independently of how context is captured or inferred, it has to be distributed among the system components (sensors, middleware, application). Some articles refer to this distribution scheme as the system *architecture*, although the term *architecture* usually comprises other things such as the system modules, repositories, sub-layers, etc. In this section, we focus solely on how context is distributed in the system.

The most common approach for distributed context-aware systems uses a centralized middleware as a broker between dispersed sensors and client applications (see Fig. 2.9a). For example, CenceMe [59] shares personal context obtained from mobile phones through an HTTP server. All users of the CenceMe application rely on this server to send and receive context information to/from other users. This approach is useful to relieve resource-constrained devices from CPU and memory-demanding tasks and simplifies the communication since the devices (sensor or application) only need to establish a channel between them and a single component (the server). However, it is a single point of failure and thereby lacks robustness. Even if the server does not fail, its scalability is limited—as more devices use the

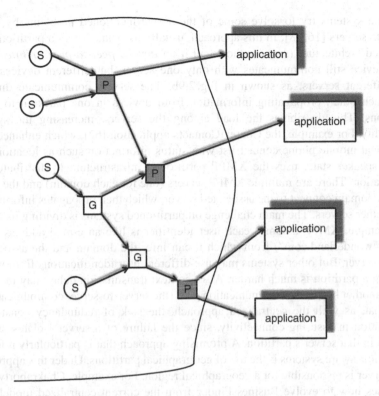

Fig. 2.8 The Solar system pushes application-specific processing into network proxies (represented by *dark squares*) that can be combined and reused by other applications (S=sensors; *white squares*=generic context processors)

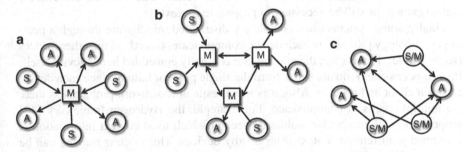

Fig. 2.9 The three types of distributed organization for context-aware systems (M, middleware; S, sensor; A, application): (**a**) centralized, (**b**) partitioned, and (**c**) peer-to-peer

system, its performance will start degrading. Also, it is not well fitted to scenarios where network connection is intermittent as it happens with mobile phones. Unless the application uses local caching mechanisms, it may stop working when the connection with the server drops.

Some systems try to solve some of the above mentioned problems by using multiple servers [16, 38]. In this approach, usually associated with a partitioned or federated architecture (some authors call it an *acyclic peer-to-peer architecture*), each device still communicates with only one server, but different devices may use different servers, as shown in Fig. 2.9b. The servers communicate directly with each other, propagating information from devices in one partition to other partitions. This distributes the load among the servers, increasing the system scalability. For example, the ContextContacts application [62], which enhances the traditional mobile phone contact list with status information such as location and phone speaker state, uses the XMPP partitioned infrastructure to distribute this information. There are multiple XMPP servers (one for each domain) and the users of each domain connect to the associated server, which then propagates information to the other servers. The main challenge on partitioned systems is dividing its users. For example, XMPP assumes each user identifier is like an e-mail address (e.g., "alice@wonderland.com") from which it can infer the domain and the associated XMPP server. But other systems may use different user identifications from which deriving a partition is much harder. Also, context transmission delay may increase due to another hop in the communication path (the server-to-server communication). Note that, as with the centralized approach, the lack of redundancy constitutes a limitation in assuring connectivity, since the failure of a server isolates all the devices in that server's partition. A promising approach that is particularly relevant to location-aware systems is the use of geographical partitions. Under this approach, each server is responsible for a geographical region. For example, Chakraborty [20] addresses how to evolve BusinessFinder from the current centralized model to a geographically partitioned model. BusinessFinder, a "Yellow Pages" application which searches vendors nearby the current user location, is particularly suited to this model, since in most cases the client and the vendor will share the same server and no extra hops will be necessary to propagate context.

Finally, some systems use a completely distributed middleware through a peer-to-peer topology [50], where each device communicates directly to the other devices (see Fig. 2.9c). In this case, the middleware is usually embedded in the device itself. Peer-to-peer systems do not suffer from the single point of failure, since each device acts as a client and a server. Also, it is more resilient to network problems as there are multiple paths to communicate. For example, the Hydrogen framework [47] proposes an architecture for mobile devices in which local context information is combined with remote context from nearby devices. This *context sharing* can be used to pair two devices with complementary information (e.g., a thermometer and a GPS receiver) communicating through Bluetooth. However, these systems have to employ complex algorithms to ensure that context information produced by the sensors is delivered to all interested applications. Contrary to centralized and partitioned models, the components of these systems are in a constant discovery process of new sensors and applications that wish to communicate with them. Also, depending on the routing algorithm, the time necessary to propagate context may increase when multiple hops are needed to connect the source and the destination nodes.

Context-aware systems that follow a decentralized (peer-to-peer) architecture are usually related to a geographical distribution of their nodes in order to provide efficient location-based services. Some examples of these systems include GHT [75] and IGM [31]. The advantage of these systems over traditional peer-to-peer architectures is that nodes know their location and the location of nearby nodes, which allows efficient geographical routing (e.g., a notification can be sent to all nodes that are within a predefined geographic region). Note that, in these systems, operations are not limited to a user local region; therefore, users can perform operations on the entire network, e.g., the user querying Indian restaurants in Dublin may be currently in New York. Operations can also be performed by proxy nodes, i.e., a node in Dublin may perform and aggregate results of other nodes in Dublin and return these results to the user in New York [31].

Typically, these systems have been applied to sensor networks or geographical service directories, where context is not tied to human behavior, thus limiting the potential scope of its applications. For example, services like "Find friends dancing near me" would be good candidates to be implemented on top of decentralized networks (where the nodes would probably be mobile phones). Also, to the best of our knowledge, none of the proposed decentralized context-aware applications to date support collaborative features.

Although most systems fall into just one of these categories, there are hybrid systems that combine different distribution models, like AwareMedia [9], an awareness tool to help hospital staff coordination. AwareMedia is developed using SIENA [16], which features a hybrid approach that mixes the partitioned and the peer-to-peer models. In SIENA, devices are distributed within partitions, with each partition having an associated server. Communication between partitions is made using server-to-server direct connections as usual. However, the devices within each partition are organized in a peer-to-peer model. Instead of communicating only with the partition server, they are also able to communicate directly between them. BikeNet [36] also implements a hybrid approach that combines a centralized model with a peer-to-peer model. Bicycle sensors may transmit context data directly to a central server or to other sensors in passing by bicycles, which are then transmitted to the central server.

2.6 Consume

After context information has been captured from sensors, inferred into higher-level data and distributed through the network, it will be consumed by client applications. In this section, we describe how client applications obtain this context information in a distributed context-aware system, categorizing the possible options and presenting examples of such options. Figure 2.10 presents a taxonomy of approaches for dealing with context information consumption.

Context-aware systems can be either push or pull-based. In *pull-based systems*, the consumer (client application) queries the component that has the information

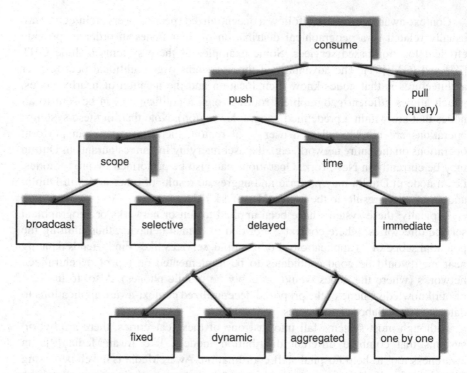

Fig. 2.10 Consume layer

(sensor or middleware) for updates. This can be done manually (e.g., the user clicks the "refresh" button) or periodically (e.g., checking for updates every 5 min). In *push-based systems*, the component that has the information is responsible for delivering it to interested client applications. The main distinction between these approaches lies on who initiates the communication. If a client application initiates the communication, the system is pull-based; otherwise it is push-based.

Pull-based mechanisms are simple to implement because the client application only has to query a certain component with a certain periodicity. In the extreme scenario, the application can simply delegate the responsibility of refreshing the information to the user. Also, this periodicity (polling interval) can change according to the application current needs. For example, an application running on a mobile phone can increase the polling interval to save battery life, when the battery power falls below a certain threshold. However, this mechanism suffers from two problems that can be critical in a context-aware system. First, context information reaches the application with a delay. In the worst case, this delay equals the polling interval. If the polling interval is defined as 5 min, there will be cases where the application receives context information from 5 min ago, compromising its usefulness. The application can minimize this disadvantage by reducing the polling interval, but then, the second problem may start occurring—most queries will be unnecessary since there is no new context information available. Since the application does not know when there will be updates, it has no alternative as to keep asking until there is new information, leading to wasted network bandwidth and CPU consumption.

Push-based mechanisms are more complex than pull-based mechanisms. Since the component that has the information is also responsible for delivering it, this component has to know how to reach every possible consumer that is interested in that information. Usually, a permanent connection with all the consumers is necessary. If the system has a large number of consumers, its performance may degrade. Furthermore, these systems have poor scalability as every new consumer degrades the performance even worse. There are two measures to overcome the scalability problem: *reduce scope* and/or *relax delivery time*. We describe these measures in the following sections.

Although the *push vs. pull* issue is mainly analyzed from the distributed systems perspective, context-aware systems raise additional challenges on deciding between both approaches. Cheverst [27] argues that applications that use push-based mechanisms may surprise the user, disrupting his current task. However, he also refers that allowing the application to present inconsistent data (as happens in the pull-based approach) may confuse the user. He tested this rationale with a location-aware visitor guide [26] that was originally designed following the pull model, whereby the onus was on the users to request the presentation of context-aware information.[2] Cheverst developed a push-based version of this application that immediately reacts to context updates (e.g., location changes) presenting the user with constantly updated information about nearby attractions. The subsequent evaluation showed that visitors were comfortable with the push-based version, because it required less effort to learn and use than the pull-based version.

2.6.1 Scope

In many context-aware systems, users are only interested in a subset of the system's available context information. For example, users of AwarePhone [8] (an application that enhances the traditional phone contact list with contextual information such as location and availability) are only interested in context updates for the people in their contact list. In this system, if person A has person B in his list of contacts, A is notified if B moves from one location to another, but other people in the system without B in their contact list are not notified. AwarePhone is built on top of the AWARE framework [8], which provides an event-based infrastructure, as long as the underlying communication channel allows it. Currently, the supported communication channels are Java RMI, PHO (special-purpose optimized channel for mobile phones), and HTTP. HTTP, due to its stateless request-response nature, is the only one that does not support push-based context propagation. ContextPhone [72] uses a similar mechanism on top of the XMPP protocol [79].

---

[2]For example, by tapping on the information button.

These are examples of *selective scope* systems, that is, systems that propagate only a subset of the available context information based on user's selection. Most context-aware systems propagate all the available context information, thus falling into the *broadcast scope* category (see Fig. 2.10).

Using scope is an effective technique to reduce the number of pushed messages in the system, thus reducing the required outbound network bandwidth on the component that has the information and improving overall scalability.

Although selective scope filtering is usually applied on the middleware layer, some systems apply the filter on the sensor. Elvin [88] introduces the concept of *quenching*, a mechanism that allows sensors to know whether client applications are interested in their information and only sending information in that case.[3]

2.6.2 Time

Another way to improve push-based systems scalability is to assume that certain context information does not need to be immediately delivered. Users tolerate some lag as long as the information does not require urgent attention. For example, a context-aware system that shows friends near me is not required to be continuously up to date. On the other hand, an application that shares current availability among a group of friends (e.g., to help decide whether a person can call a certain friend without interrupting anything) loses its usefulness if context information is not propagated as soon as possible.

These issues have been studied in the context of *optimistic replication algorithms*. Such algorithms increase availability and scalability of distributed data sharing systems by allowing replica contents to diverge in the short term [80]. Distributed context-aware systems are, in fact, a large distributed database of context information. In addition, most of them use a crude form of single-master replication—all updates originate at the master and then are propagated to other replicas, or slaves. Applying this general definition to context-aware systems, we have context information replicated among multiple nodes with sensors acting as masters and end-user applications acting as slaves. Since sensors are the only components that *write* context information, these systems do not suffer from conflicting updates, which is one of the main problems found in optimistic replication algorithms.

Improved scalability is just one of the advantages of using delayed context propagation. This technique also allows for greater availability and network flexibility, working well over slow, unreliable, or intermittent connection links. Such property is essential in mobile environments in which devices can be synchronized only occasionally. For example, Riché [77] proposes a system for managing user context

---

[3]In fact, Elvin is not specific to context-aware applications and quenching can be applied to any publish-subscribe system.

across multiple devices that survives intermittent device connectivity by applying optimistic replication techniques.

In spite of this, the majority of distributed context-aware systems use the immediate approach pushing context information to end-user applications as soon as possible.

Delayed context propagation can be further categorized based on the *interval between updates* and the *amount of information transmitted on each update* (see Fig. 2.10):

- **Fixed vs. dynamic**—Systems which postpone context propagation must decide when to actually push the updates. This decision can be made based on a fixed criteria such as time period (push the update every x seconds) or amount of retained information (push the update when there is more than x Kbytes of context information). For example, ReConMUC [6] uses both criteria to improve the scalability of a context-aware IM application.

   Context propagation can also occur using a dynamic criteria, such as the importance or urgency of the context information. For example, consider a location-based system which propagates context more frequently if the recipient is geographically near the origin. In this system, people in the same building could receive context information from each other almost immediately while context information from people in the vicinity, but not in the building, would be received with a certain delay.[4]

- **Aggregated vs. one-by-one**—Since there is a delay in context propagation, information must be retained and may start accumulating. So, when the system decides to push the update, there may be a considerable number of messages to transmit. The most simple approach is to transmit the messages one-by-one, as would be the case if there was not any delay. However, it can also be extremely inefficient.

   Consider the case of a moving person carrying a GPS-enabled device constantly updating his location to his friends. Consider also that this system uses a delayed push technique to improve scalability, with a fixed period of 1 min (i.e., a maximum delay of 1 min between update propagation). During each minute, the system may accumulate a large number of location positions (since the person is moving). If, after each period, the system transmits the location messages one-by-one, it consumes network bandwidth without necessity because, in fact, only the last location is relevant to his friends. In this case, the system could aggregate all the location positions in just one (the last). Even when all the retained messages are relevant, they can still be aggregated in one big message, achieving higher levels of compression and much less round-trips in the connection path [6].

   Note that, in context-aware related literature, the term "aggregation" is often associated with the combination of information from different sensors, along

---

[4]Context from people outside the vicinity would not be received at all, but this falls into the selective scope approach.

with conflict resolution. Such *multiple sensor aggregation* should not be confused with the aforementioned aggregation which is specifically related to accumulated messages on systems that use a delayed push approach.

2.7 Summary

We started this chapter with some basic definitions regarding context-aware systems. In particular, we say that a system is context-aware if it uses context to provide relevant information and/or services to the user. Then, we presented a taxonomy for distributed context-aware systems which is based on the following main layers: capture, infer, distribute, and consume. These layers are traversed by context data, from the moment it is acquired from sensors in raw format to the moment it is consumed by the end-user application. For each one of these layers we detailed the several techniques that can be used.

Chapter 3
Systems

Abstract Once we have defined a taxonomy for distributed context-aware systems (in the previous chapter), we analyze some of the most relevant systems in this area, providing an overview of their functionalities and architecture and classifying them according to the previously described taxonomy. The chapter concludes with a table that summarizes, for each described system, the solution used regarding each layer (capture, infer, distribute, and consume).

3.1 GUIDE

GUIDE [26] provides city visitors with a hand-portable context-aware tourist guide. The system has been successfully deployed in the city of Lancaster and is publicly available to visitors who wish to explore the city. The city's major attractions are covered with a cell-based wireless communications infrastructure (based on the 802.11 WiFi protocol). Each wireless access point (AP) has an associated *cell server* and is responsible for (i) broadcasting location beacons to provide positioning information and (ii) disseminating both static and dynamic information to mobile GUIDE units. Each one of these *cell servers* has local storage capabilities and acts as a proxy cache to the central GUIDE web server (see Fig. 3.1).

Each mobile device stores the user profile (preferred language, user's name, etc.) and, combined with location information provided by the location beacons, provides relevant information to users about nearby touristic attractions.

GUIDE uses a purpose-built information model [25] that represents places, such as attractions and key buildings, within the city. This model is translated into HTML by a local web server resident in every GUIDE mobile device.

This system had an interesting evolution since it started as a distributed non-collaborative system and was subsequently extended to support collaboration. In particular, two collaborative features were implemented: (i) create a comment and rating for association with a particular attraction and (ii) realize that another GUIDE

P. Ferreira and P. Alves, *Distributed Context-Aware Systems*, SpringerBriefs in Computer Science, DOI 10.1007/978-3-319-04882-6_3, © The Author(s) 2014

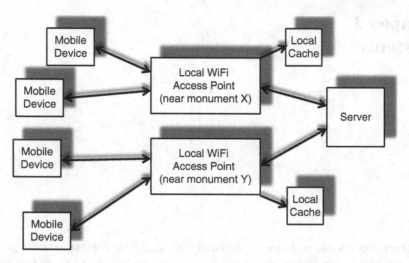

Fig. 3.1 GUIDE architecture

user is (or has recently been) physically located at a particular attraction. In order to provide these features, GUIDE mobile devices were changed to periodically acknowledge their location to the APs, in order to share their location to other users. To protect their privacy, users are able to specify if they do not mind having their location recorded but wish to remain anonymous (in that case, the user identifier that is passed to the server is a random one) and if they do not wish to have their location recorded at all.

Since acknowledging every location beacon would result in large network bandwidth consumption, only 1 in 10 beacons is acknowledged by the mobile device.

In summary, GUIDE captures context (location) through physical sensors (WiFi). Nearby attraction names are inferred from the IP address of the corresponding AP, in the server (middleware). Context information is distributed through a centralized topology with an intermediate caching layer that reduces the dependency between the mobile devices and the central server. Information about touristic attractions is obtained by querying the server (pull), but the location of the mobile devices is detected using a selective, periodic, push-based approach; it is selective because the location beacons are only emitted to a subset of all the mobile devices in the city (only those in the AP wireless range); it is periodic (fixed delay) because the beacons are pushed to the mobile devices periodically. As already noted, only 1 in 10 location beacons is acknowledged by the mobile device, which can be considered a form of context aggregation.

3.2 UbiqMuseum

UbiqMuseum [15] is similar to GUIDE but is intended to be used inside a building (usually a museum). This system provides relevant information to museum visitors through mobile devices based on proximity to pieces of art, using Bluetooth to give proximity in-buildings context. The short wireless range of Bluetooth technology is suitable to much finer-grained location than WiFi and, unlike GPS, works inside buildings.

UbiqMuseum's architecture features an edge wireless network based on Bluetooth technology used by mobile devices integrated with a core network based on a fixed Ethernet and wireless 802.11b LAN. The core network connects mobile clients with servers. The system considers three types of software entities (see Fig. 3.2): client applications, museum information points (MIPs), and the central data server. MIPs are associated with one or more pieces of art or objects.

A mobile client, while wondering around the museum, continuously searches for new MIPs through Bluetooth inquiry process (Service Discovery Protocol). Then, mobile clients send the user profile to the MIP, also using Bluetooth. The MIP forwards the request to the central server (the authors do not specify which protocol is used in this communication) and receives information about that piece of art, which updates its local cache and forwards to the mobile client.

This system does not provide any collaborative feature and context (location) is never persisted, so there is no need for privacy mechanisms.

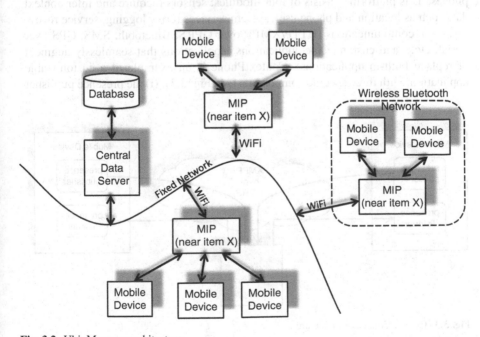

Fig. 3.2 UbiqMuseum architecture

In summary, UbiqMuseum is very similar to GUIDE: physical sensors (Bluetooth) capture location information, which is inferred into pieces of art by the server (middleware) and distributed along a centralized topology (again, since the MIPs can cache information, the dependency of the central server is reduced). The main difference w.r.t. GUIDE is the location detection mechanism, which is pull-based. The mobile clients are responsible for periodically discovering and querying nearby MIPs.

3.3   ContextContacts

ContextContacts [62] enhances the traditional mobile phone contact list with clues of the current situation of others, such as location, time spent in that location, phone speaker state, and number of persons near the phone. The goal is to help the caller to decide if the callee can be interrupted and, in that case, which communication channel to use.

Unlike the previous examples, this application captures other types of context besides location, like phone activity (speaker and vibrator state, calls), sensing how many people are nearby using Bluetooth, etc. Location is obtained through the GSM cell ID.

From the architectural perspective, the system is built on top of ContextPhone [72], a generic platform to help develop context-aware applications for mobile phones. This platform consists of four modules: sensors (acquire and infer context data such as location and phone use), system services (error logging, service recovery, etc.), communications (HTTP/XMPP over GPRS, Bluetooth, SMS, GPS over Serial, etc.), and customizable applications (applications that seamlessly augment or replace built-in applications). ContextPhone is an example of a customizable application, with three specific components (see Fig. 3.3): (i) the presence publisher

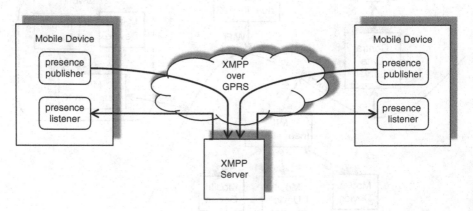

Fig. 3.3 ContextContacts architecture

which gathers and sends relevant sensory data to other users via XMPP; (ii) the presence listener which receives sensory data from others and integrates it into the applications' user interface, and (iii) application customizations such as the adaptation of the built-in contacts list application.

Although Bluetooth is used, it cannot be considered a communication channel since its purpose is to gather sensory data related to people nearby. All communication is done using XMPP push-based presence protocol. This protocol establishes a two-way permanent channel (TCP) between the client and the server and propagates presence information based on a publish-subscribe model [65].

Since this system provides collaborative features to help synchronization of a group, its user's privacy must be preserved. In ContextContacts, privacy is managed using self-awareness mechanisms: the application provides a separate view showing exactly how others see the user at the moment. However, the only way to control what is revealed is to switch off the application.

In summary, although the system captures a wider range of context information (not only location), it is still mostly captured through physical sensors. Location is inferred from the GSM cell ID by the client application associated with the phone being used. Thus, the client application infers the higher-level location information (e.g., city) before propagating that information for the other devices. Since ContextContacts relies on XMPP protocol, it benefits from its partitioned architecture, with the advantages outlined in Sect. 2.5. Also, since XMPP uses a publish-subscribe model, the system is push-based, with immediate and selective propagation (context is only propagated to the users that are on the contact list, not every user in the system).

3.4 BusinessFinder

BusinessFinder [20] may be viewed as a "Live Yellow Pages" service that factors in the actual mobility of both the requester (the customer seeking a service) and the vendors (e.g., the electrician or plumber offering the service) to perform on-demand matching. The system is targeted to *nomadic* vendors whose location is always changing as opposed to traditional local static services like restaurants and gas stations. Users trigger the system by sending an SMS like "Find me the nearest plumber."

To increase adoption, BusinessFinder does not require a client application to be installed in mobile phones. Therefore, it does not have direct access to mobile phone sensors. Instead, it relies on the services provided by the mobile phone operator infrastructure, either using a Parlay Gateway (a generic interface to common mobile services such as location, SMS processing, and call control) or a SIP Presence Server. The interaction with these interfaces can be query-based (pull) or push-based (change-triggered notifications). BusinessFinder also maintains a database of vendors' profiles including skills, availability, and rating.

The system was implemented following the centralized model (a single Presence Server or Parlay Gateway interacting with a single Location Server). The authors intend to research an alternative distributed architecture, partitioned by geographical areas. In this architecture, all vendors resident in a specific zone transmit their presence updates to the corresponding server. The major challenge in this model occurs when there are no available vendors in the local server and the query needs to be routed to alternative servers from nearby areas. The authors propose a *resource-aware query routing (RAQR)* algorithm [19] that avoids broadcasting or query flooding by maintaining a *gradient-offer* table in each server that is near resource exhaustion. This *gradient-offer* table is a local representation of the available resources on nearby servers and can be used to reserve certain remote resources anticipating local resource exhaustion.

Regarding privacy, although the system continually keeps track of its user location, that information is never directly revealed unless a match occurs between client and vendor. Even in that case, all subsequent interactions are explicit and identities are only revealed in the last step—upon matching the system sends an SMS to the requester like "Vendor at distance 10.85 kms is available. Reply Connect Yes/No."

In summary, BusinessFinder uses the physical sensors associated with the mobile phone (although indirectly through the cellular operator infrastructure). Inference is provided by the cellular operator infrastructure which is organized in a centralized architecture. Context can be consumed using either the pull mechanism or the push mechanism. In the later case, the events are broadcasted immediately.

3.5   AwarePhone

AwarePhone [8] is similar to ContextContacts in the way it augments the traditional phone contact list with richer context information, but it is implemented over a different architecture—the AWARE framework. One of the interesting characteristics of this framework is its support for direct communication (e.g., IM) besides context propagation. In fact, the core idea in the AWARE architecture is to combine CSCW system components for providing social awareness among collaborating users with ubiquitous computing components for obtaining context awareness.

In particular, AwarePhone is an application for mobile phones that displays a contact list with enhanced context information (personal status, activity, and location) and supports simple text messaging. It uses diverse sensors such as WiFi, IR, Bluetooth, Calendar (from which the current activity is inferred), and Status (virtual sensor: the user manually sets its status). Location can be inferred from WiFi, IR, or Bluetooth depending on the environment.

The AWARE architecture is divided into four layers (see Fig. 3.4):

- **Monitor and Actuator Layer**—This is the sensor layer. Currently, AWARE supports some location sensors (WiFi, Bluetooth, IR beacon, RFID), an activity

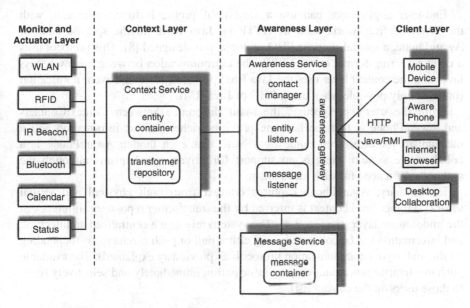

Fig. 3.4 AWARE architecture

virtual sensor based on the calendar, and a personal status sensor manually set by the user.

- **Context Layer**—This layer manages context information about relevant entities in the real world, such as people, places, and things and distributes this information to the awareness layer using either a request-response or a publish-subscribe pattern.
- **Awareness Layer**—This layer has three responsibilities: (i) maintain information about users subscribing to the AWARE system, and about whom they want to maintain social awareness; (ii) handle connections to clients using different protocols, reply to their requests, and know how to notify them about relevant events; and (iii) manage a message broker that enables users to post messages to each other. The message broker is an optional component which can be replaced by the standard SMS service, but the authors claim that its "embed ability" provides a smoother transition from context awareness to direct communication.
- **Client Layer**—This layer includes all end-user applications that use this framework, including a phone client, a desktop client, and an Internet (browser) client. This layer communicates with the awareness layer through a gateway which is able to transform protocol-specific requests into internal AWARE API calls.

The awareness layer uses the context infrastructure by connecting to a Context Service and registering itself as a listener to relevant entities. Then, it starts receiving notifications of relevant changes. Applications running on devices can now treat these events appropriately, i.e., updating the user interface or notifying users.

End-user applications can use a variety of protocols to communicate with the AWARE framework, such as HTTP or Java RMI. In the specific case of AwarePhone, a special-purpose PHO protocol was designed [8]. This protocol uses a compact string format over TCP/IP. The communication between the awareness layer and the context layer uses the Java RMI protocol. Note that event notification (push) is only possible when using PHO or Java RMI.

From the user's perspective, the main difference between ContextContacts and AwarePhone is that the last one provides richer context information and a mechanism for direct communication. Note that even though AwarePhone is a collaborative system, there is no support for privacy mechanisms although the authors refer a need for such mechanisms.

In summary, AwarePhone captures context from both physical and virtual sensors. Higher-level context is inferred by the transformer repository (inference at the middleware layer; see Fig. 3.4). The system relies on a centralized architecture, and information can be consumed using either pull or push mechanisms (depending on the underlying communication protocol, as previously explained). The available push mechanism propagates context information immediately and selectively (only to those users on the contact list).

3.6 CenceMe

CenceMe [59] exploits off-the-shelf sensor-enabled mobile phones to automatically infer people's sensing presence (e.g., dancing at a party with friends) and then shares this presence through social network portals such as Facebook. While systems like ContextContacts and AwarePhone are much more focused on productivity features (e.g., reducing the chance of interrupting someone), CenceMe is focused on connecting people by sharing their personal status in a social network, usually for entertainment purposes.

The personal status is very sophisticated and goes well beyond traditional location. The phone's microphone is used to capture audio samples from the environment (e.g., detecting if the user is in a dance club) and the built-in accelerometer is used to infer current activity like sitting and walking. Bluetooth, GPS, and camera are also used (the last one to take random photos of the environment surrounding the user). Richer sensors such as microphone and accelerometer imply more complex inference engines, using CPU-intensive operations such as discrete Fourier transform (DFT) and machine learning algorithms.

CenceMe is implemented in a traditional centralized architecture, where an application installed on the mobile phone transmits and receives context information to/from an HTTP server (see Fig. 3.5). However, this system proposes an interesting twist over other similar systems called *split-level classification*. The idea is to push some of the context-inference process to the mobile phone, and some to the server, in order to improve scalability. This architecture offers some advantages: (i) supports *customized tags* (any activity, gesture, or audio that the user can bind to a personal

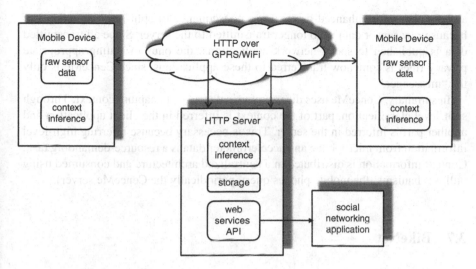

Fig. 3.5 CenceMe architecture

meeting, such as drawing an imaginary circle with the phone to indicate "going to lunch"); (ii) provides resiliency to cellular/WiFi dropouts, by computing and buffering context information when there is no radio coverage; (iii) minimizes the sensor data the phone sends to the server improving the system efficiency by only uploading classification-derived primitives rather than higher bandwidth raw sensed data; (iv) reduces energy consumed by the phone by merging consecutive uploads; and (v) eliminates the need to send raw sensor data to the back-end, enhancing the user's privacy.

The protocol used for communication is HTTP over WiFi or GPRS, depending on network availability. Data exchange is initiated by the phone at timed intervals whenever the phone has primitives to upload. The phone also periodically pings the server with control messages. Messages from the server are piggybacked on both phone- initiated messages. To extend the battery life of the phone when running the CenceMe application, data upload and sensing components may be slightly delayed, minimizing sampling and context propagation while maintaining the application's responsiveness. Right now, this delay must be set manually by each user. Also, although it increases the battery lifetime of the phone, it was detected to have a negative impact on the performance of the classifiers.

It is noteworthy that split-level classification allows for some aggregation of messages. By uploading to the server higher-level context data instead of raw sensor data, the application is effectively aggregating context without losing relevant context information. Also, to reduce the number of data cellular connections, the application merges consecutive uploads to the server.

In any system with social features, user's privacy must be assured. CenceMe includes a privacy setting GUI that allows the user to enable or disable the five sensing modalities by user with whom they are willing to share some information. The authors also refer enhanced privacy as a consequence of split-level classification, because raw sensor data is no longer transmitted to the server. Since all transmitted data is published to social network applications, the onus of setting appropriate privacy rules is somehow transferred to these applications, since CenceMe is only the "messenger."

In summary, CenceMe uses diverse physical sensors to capture context. Through split-level classification, part of the context is inferred in the client application and another part is inferred in the server. This is necessary because inferring high-level information from microphone and accelerometer data is a resource-demanding task. Context information is distributed in a centralized architecture and consumed using pull mechanisms (the mobile phones query periodically the CenceMe server).

3.7   BikeNet

BikeNet [36] was developed by the same group that developed CenceMe to improve the cycling experience with miscellaneous sensors attached to the bike. During a ride, these sensors continuously capture environmental and personal data such as current speed, average speed, distance traveled, path slope, heart rate, and galvanic skin response. This data is transmitted to a central server for further visualization and comparison with friends/competitors through a web-based portal.

The system is organized into three tiers: the back-end server tier, the sensor access point (SAP), and the mobile sensor tier. The mobile sensor tier includes all the sensors attached to the bicycle, including an accelerometer, thermistor, photodiode, and microphone. The SAP tier acts as a gateway from the sensor tier to the back-end server. SAPs can be static and wired directly to the Internet (e.g., wireless 802.11 router) or can be mobile using a wide area radio access network (e.g., mobile phone with GSM/GPRS). Static SAPs may be distributed across a cycling route. When the bicycle comes within the range of these SAPs, sensor data is uploaded to the back-end server. This is the default mode, where cyclists go on trips, collect sensed data, and upload their data when they return home. Obviously, this implies a delay between the time the sensor data packet is generated and the time this packet reaches the central server.

This delay can be reduced using a mobile SAP. If the rider goes cycling with his mobile phone, it can be used as a real-time interface between the sensors and the central server. In this case, the only delay is the time it takes for the sensor data to be transmitted over the GPRS connection, and it is possible to follow the ride in real time using the web portal (e.g., updating the current location on a map). In any case, BikeNet distributes context information using a centralized topology, using either a *delayed sensing mode* or an *immediate continuous sensing mode*.

This system introduces an interesting networking solution that takes advantage of the opportunities that arise as a result of the uncontrolled mobility of the cyclists, using a *muling* exchange protocol (which is in fact a simplified epidemic protocol [32]). In the muling exchange, sensed data is transferred between mobile sensors outside the wireless range of either a mobile or static SAP. This occurs when two bicycles equipped with BikeNet pass by each other. The sensors of one bike are able to detect the presence of another bike and establish a direct wireless connection between them. The idea is to collect sensed data from other bicycles found along the ride, in addition to our own data. When entering the wireless range of static SAP, all data is uploaded to the server. That is, the first bicycle to stop uploads sensed data of the other (still running) bicycles, decreasing the already mentioned delay that occurs when using static SAPs. In addition, if one of the bicycles participating in the muling exchange has access to a mobile SAP (when the cyclist brought its mobile phone), sensed data is uploaded immediately, further reducing the delay. This opportunistic protocol creates, in fact, small peer-to-peer networks that allow the system to efficiently work in disconnected or intermittent clients. Note that, in this system, only one-hop muling is allowed—sensed data can be replicated but replication of mulled data is not supported. The reason argued by the authors is that if unlimited replication was allowed, it would be impossible for the client to know the number of copies of its data in the system.

3.8 Tickertape

Tickertape [38] is a desktop application that displays notifications on topics that the user has previously subscribed to. Its interface consists of a single resizable rectangular window, showing small, color-coded messages scrolling from right to left. Context is propagated using Elvin [87], a generic notification service following the publish-subscribe paradigm. Users can subscribe to groups of messages (e.g., "work" messages) and can filter messages within those groups based on their content (e.g., messages that contain the word "tickertape").

Unlike the already mentioned context-aware systems, Tickertape relies solely on virtual sensors, mainly information sources (Usenet news, CNN stories, etc.) and chat messages. Since these sensors produce high-level information there is no need for an inference engine in this system.

As already referred, Tickertape is developed on top of Elvin, a content-based notification server using a partitioned architecture, as shown in Fig. 3.6. Multiple Elvin Daemons (servers) listen to events coming from Event Producers and deliver them to interested clients, based on their subscriptions. Communication between clients and servers is asynchronous and can use a variety of protocols ranging from raw TCP and UDP to HTTP and HTTPS.

From a collaborative point of view, Tickertape provides mechanisms for shared context awareness in a group of people but also for direct communication (clicking on the Tickertape opens a pop-up dialog where users can write messages).

In summary, Tickertape captures all context information from virtual sensors, it does not use any inference engine, it relies in a partitioned architecture, and context information is pushed immediately and selectively (based on user-defined filters) to the client application.

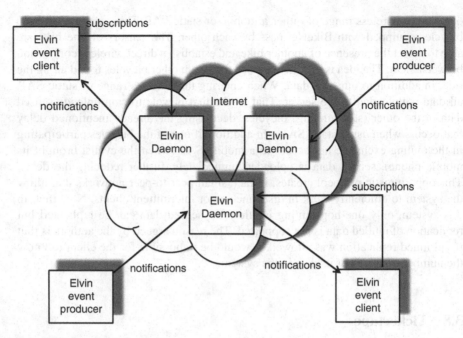

Fig. 3.6 The Elvin architecture for content-based routing

3.9 NESSIE

NESSIE [67] is an awareness environment for cooperative settings in an office. A NESSIE client application runs on a PC, presenting events taking place in the office and showing locations of others in places of interest (e.g., shared information or social places). Information can be presented through multiple interfaces like simple windows with events listings, background images and sounds, or Tickertape-like [38] applications. In short, NESSIE matches user-defined filters with context information captured in an office, mainly through virtual sensors that detect modifications on shared artifacts (e.g., documents).

NESSIE uses mostly virtual sensors, although some physical sensors have also been integrated. Some virtual sensors allow the application to know the *information space location* of every user. *Information space location* refers to a virtual location that can be visited by users, like a web page, a document, or a virtual world's room. In addition, physical sensors like video image motion recognition sensor, infrared motion detection sensor, and acoustic microphones are used to detect the presence of people in a room.

NESSIE follows a traditional client-server architecture, in combination with an event database. The server supports two methods of production and provision of events: asynchronous (pull) server interaction (HTTP calls) and synchronous (push) notifications based on registered interest profiles by the NESSIE client

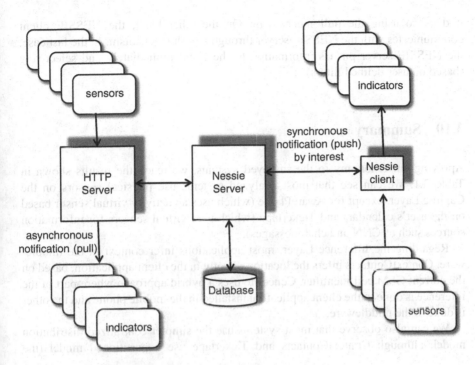

Fig. 3.7 NESSIE architecture

(see Fig. 3.7). It also introduces the concept of *Indicator*, an application with a graphical user interface (GUI) that shows context information. Even though sensors may communicate directly with the NESSIE client (i.e., without going through the NESSIE server), we believe the most common case to be sensors communicating with the server using the pull mechanism and then the server propagates this information to interested NESSIE clients (based on user profiles) using the push mechanism.

With respect to inference, the NESSIE server includes an event transformation module that allows the transformation of submitted events.

Regarding privacy, NESSIE events can include an access control attribute listing the users who are allowed to receive that event. Also, to prevent misuse, NESSIE provides a *reciprocity* mechanism—it discloses the users who have registered interest in the events produced by a certain user ("when you see me, I see you"). This information is useful not only for the support of reciprocity; it further informs a user about the list of people who will become aware of a certain activity. This is important when a certain reaction is expected on the activity that raised the event.

In summary, NESSIE uses both physical and virtual sensors to capture context information which may be subject to further inference in the server. Data is propagated through a centralized architecture and uses both push and pull mechanisms. If the client application (*Indicator*) consumes information from the HTTP server, it does so using the pull mechanism. On the other hand, the NESSIE client communicates with the NESSIE server through a push mechanism. In the last case, the NESSIE server pushes information to the client immediately and selectively (based on user-defined filters).

3.10　Summary

Applying our taxonomy to the surveyed systems, we reach the results shown in Table 3.1. We can see that most analyzed systems use physical sensors on the Capture Layer, except for AwarePhone (which uses an activity virtual sensor based on the user's calendar) and Tickertape (which uses virtual sensors for information sources such as CNN and chat messages).

Regarding the Inference Layer, most applications infer context in the middleware. ContextContacts infers the location directly in the client application, based on the current GSM cell identifier. CenceMe uses a hybrid approach where part of the inference is done in the client application installed in the mobile phone and the other is done in the middleware.

We can also observe that most systems use the simpler centralized distribution model, although ContextContacts and Tickertape use a partitioned model (the

Table 3.1 Classification of the surveyed systems

	Capture	Infer	Distribute	Consume
GUIDE	Physical	Middleware	Centralized[a]	Pull (attraction information)/ push: selective, fixed delay (location)
UbiqMuseum	Physical	Middleware	Centralized[a]	Pull
ContextContacts	Physical	Client application	Partitioned	Push: selective, immediate
BusinessFinder	Physical	Middleware	Centralized[b]	Push: broadcast, immediate
CenceMe	Physical	Middleware/ client application[c]	Centralized	Pull
AwarePhone	Physical/ virtual	Middleware	Centralized	Pull/ push: selective, immediate
BikeNet	Physical	Middleware	Centralized/ peer-to-peer	Pull
Tickertape	Virtual	N/A	Partitioned	Push: selective, immediate
NESSIE	Physical virtual	Middleware	Centralized	Pull/ push: selective, immediate

[a] Since the location inference is based on multiple access points (either WiFi or Bluetooth) with a caching mechanism, these systems may be considered semi-partitioned but they must rely on a central server, at least while the caches are empty

[b] The authors are planning a partitioned version of BusinessFinder

[c] This system uses split-level classification: some classification is executed in the phone and other in the back-end servers (middleware)

former using XMPP and the latter using Elvin as their underlying messaging infrastructure). BikeNet uses a hybrid model that combines the centralized approach with a peer-to-peer approach (the muling exchange protocol).

Finally, systems are very diverse in how they consume information. Some of them, such as ContextContacts, BusinessFinder, and Tickertape, use a push approach while others such as UbiqMuseum and BikeNet use a pull approach. The remaining applications use a mix between the two models. Of the applications that use a push model, the majority opted for selective immediate propagation, with only one implementing a broadcast model (BusinessFinder) and another implementing a fixed delay propagation instead of an immediate one (although it was just a periodic beacon to infer the location). In fact, we can observe that none of analyzed systems uses a delayed propagation approach in spite of the advantages presented in Sect. 2.6.2.

Chapter 4
Privacy

Abstract The issue of privacy is well known and, for obvious reasons, distributed context-aware systems are not an exception. As a matter of fact, people are sensitive about revealing their location or activities (and other types of context information) which are often transmitted by such context-aware systems. In addition, such transmission is often done without requiring a specific user action, in order to increase the usability of such systems. In this chapter we define what privacy means within the realm of distributed context-aware systems; then, we describe the several privacy management techniques available: privacy policies, data perturbation, anonymization, and lookup notification.

4.1 Introduction

As already mentioned, in recent years, we have been watching a tremendous growth of available personal sensing devices such as the iPhone and Android mobile phones. These devices have come to include multiple sensors such as GPS, WiFi/3G, accelerometer, and light sensor and can run a variety of applications. In a sense, the "pervasive" world envisioned by Mark Weiser in 1995 [96], where devices integrate seamlessly into their users everyday life, is becoming a reality.

However, this seamless integration creates important privacy issues. People are sensitive about revealing their location or activities, but such context-aware systems often transmit these and other types of context information without requiring a specific user action, in order to increase their usability. For example, CenceMe [59] transmits periodically the current user's location to a group of friends. It would not make sense to ask the user permission before each transmission and users are comfortable with automatic transmissions because they have previously defined with whom they are willing to share their location. In context-aware systems used by large communities, this may not be the case. Users who easily share their location among their friends will probably reject opening up this information to the whole community, because they do not trust the recipients of that information. Still, community context-aware systems can provide immense value to their users (e.g., traffic congestion), so techniques to protect users' privacy in these systems must be employed. Clearly, the main challenge here lies on providing a fair balance between loss of privacy (what we send) and value added by the service provider (what we receive back).

Although previous research on this topic has mainly focused on the specific issues of location privacy (the ability to prevent other parties from learning one's current or past location [10, 90]), we analyze privacy management techniques that are suitable for all kinds of context-aware systems.

4.2 Definition of Privacy

Within the realm of distributed context-aware systems, the major privacy concerns pertain to the distribution of personal context to others. In this sense, we can turn to Westin's [98] definition of privacy as it is quite appropriate: *the claim of individuals, groups or institutions to determine for themselves when, how, and to what extent information about them is communicated to others.* Oyomno [63] further categorizes this definition into three properties that are essential to achieve privacy:

- **solitude**—freedom from observation or surveillance, that is, the power to prevent current or past personal context from being visible to others;
- **anonymity**—freedom from being identified in public, that is, the power to prevent others from relating context information with the actual person involved;
- **reservation**—freedom to withdraw from communication, that is, the power to interrupt personal context propagation, at any time.

Note that these properties do not map into binary (*on* or *off*) behaviors–they represent a spectrum of options that are adapted to each situation. In some situations, a person might allow others to surveil his actions (e.g., cameras in a supermarket to prevent robbery), but in other situations, that would be unbearable (e.g., cameras on his bedroom).

In fact, social psychology studies emphasize the dynamic nature of privacy, which is therefore characterized as a dynamic process of negotiating the boundary between the individual and the environment [5]. These studies also provided the background that allowed Raento [72] to provide a different set of properties for privacy-enabled systems:

- **Control**—One must be able to control the type and extent of information revealed to others, but that is typically decided dynamically according to situationally arising needs and demands. These dynamics greatly complicate the development of control mechanisms. Consolvo [28] showed that although the most important factor in disclosure is the identity of the asker or observer, there are no static rules that can decide what is revealed but that is instead completely situation-dependent.

- **Accountability**—The act of disclosing information usually implies making its recipients accountable for actions that use that information. In fact, the discloser of information may perceive breaches of implicit or explicit agreements on using revealed information and holds the other person accountable for those actions. The multiple layers introduced by distributed context-aware systems [45] increase the distance between the discloser of information and its recipients, making it much more difficult to understand the implications of such disclosure.
- **Plausible deniability**—When being asked about something private, a person must be able to plausibly deny noticing or understanding the question instead of appearing to refuse to answer. Deniability is a clear component of mediated disclosure. For example, teenagers do not always answer their mobile phones, claiming that they did not hear the ringing or that the battery was dead; this is plausible for mobile phones due to their unreliability but it can happen in direct face-to-face communication as well, when someone pretends to misunderstand the question or answers vaguely.
- **Reciprocity**—The disclosure of personal information is normally not one-sided, but mostly symmetrical: the amount of disclosure from A to B is strongly related to the amount of disclosure from B to A. Studies have shown that reciprocity in self-disclosure between partners is necessary for building of trust and deepening of relationship [78].
- **Utility**— On a more sociological point of view, there are important questions that must be answered, related to the utility of private data. For example, can the utility of private data be measured and traded? This is a very hard problem as the capabilities of future information systems are highly unpredictable. For example, nobody in 1981 knew that their newsgroup postings would be indexed and easily searchable at Google Groups.

Even though these properties are tied to sociological behavior, they provide interesting hints for privacy management techniques to include in context-aware systems. For example, we can predict now that *control* probably requires some kind of *privacy policy* and that *plausible deniability* may lead to *data perturbation* techniques. In the next section, we describe these techniques in finer detail.

4.3 Privacy Management Techniques

Privacy management techniques can be categorized into four main types (see Fig. 4.1): privacy policies, data perturbation, anonymization, and lookup notification. We start by broadly describing each one, and afterwards we delve into specific techniques for each category:

- **Privacy policies**—Applications using this technique allow the user (the context discloser) to provide rules (privacy policies) that define to whom and to what extent is his information revealed to others. This is the most common technique on both academic and industry social applications (e.g., Facebook, Twitter) and it

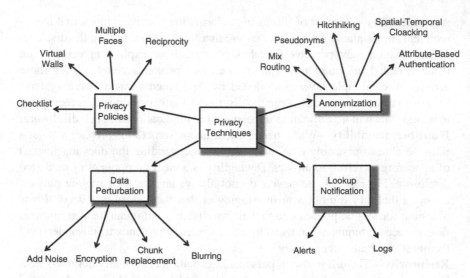

Fig. 4.1 Privacy management techniques

is tied to both Raento's *control* (although not as dynamic as the original definition implies) and *accountability*. Achieving accountability is probably the reason why this technique has been widely adopted, because it clears all the responsibilities of the service supplier from a judicial viewpoint. However, this approach has revealed multiple problems: it is cumbersome for users to specify fine-grained policies and users are not particularly good at it [30].

- **Data perturbation**—This type of technique consists on transforming or partially omitting information before being delivered to the context consumer, in such a way that it is impossible to reconstruct the original message while still keeping (some of) its usefulness. This technique may be used for effective *plausible deniability*: since the information that reaches the recipient is incomplete, the user is able to provide multiple explanations to fill in the gaps without losing credibility.

- **Anonymization**—Using this technique, the information is delivered intact to context consumers except for its author, which is removed or replaced with one that cannot be used to infer the real author. This technique is very effective: if there is no identity associated with the information, privacy is no longer an issue. Anonymization is widely used on many virtual communication tools (e.g., IRC, Forums, Wikis, Second Life), but it is prone to abuses (trolling) [89] and is being dismissed by recent social applications such as Facebook, Twitter, and LinkedIn. Also, most modern social applications include some kind of reputation management directly connected to the user's identity that rewards those who provide more personal information, effectively reducing the anonymity factor. Nevertheless, for large community social applications which gather information with the sole purpose of providing statistics (e.g., obesity control), anonymization is still very used.

- **Lookup notification**—This technique consists of providing the user with information of who has consumed his context information and when. This can occur in real time (the user is alerted that someone is consuming his context information) or *a posteriori* by keeping a log of who has seen which information. Unlike the other three techniques, which are applied before data is delivered, this technique is applied after data delivery (i.e., after a potential privacy breach) so it is usually combined with other techniques. However, it can still be a very powerful privacy mechanism. Firstly, it prevents repeated privacy breaches (e.g., due to privacy policy misconfiguration). Secondly, it creates a psychological barrier to potential privacy intruders, as they know their intrusion will be notified. Thirdly, it gives more confidence to the context provider, allowing him to use the application with less stress. This last point illustrates again the already mentioned (and desirable) *control* property.

We now detail each of these categories describing their specific techniques.

4.3.1 Privacy Policies

Privacy policies consist of a set of rules defined by the information discloser that control who is allowed to consume the information and when. Since setting rules is usually a cumbersome task, most techniques focus on providing simpler mechanisms for doing so, increasing usability and user satisfaction. There are several approaches as follows (see Fig. 4.1): checklist, virtual walls, multiple faces, and reciprocity.

4.3.1.1 Checklist

This is, by far, the most used technique for implementing privacy policies. It presents the user with a checklist of types of information (e.g., personal bio, photos, location), asking the user to choose who is allowed to see that information. This technique does not scale well neither with increasing types of information nor with a large number of potential consumers. For example, on popular social networking application Facebook, this checklist includes more than 20 topics which users have to decide with whom to share. This leads users to not changing the default privacy settings, oblivious to consequent privacy loss implications. In fact, Gross [42] found that only 1.2 % of Facebook users changed the default privacy settings for profile searchability.

4.3.1.2 Virtual Walls

Kapadia [51] proposes this technique as a solution to user difficulties in defining fine-grained privacy policies. The idea is to set up user-defined policies based on the concept of walls around physical places where sensors are deployed. These walls can be configured using a GUI and feature a three-level permission scheme: *transparent, translucent,* and *opaque.* Sensor readings are named "footprints" and can be personal (when they identify the person, like an image or speech recording) or general (related to the environment, like temperature readings). Then, a simple matrix is used to match these two dimensions: transparent walls propagate all footprints, translucent walls propagate only general footprints, and opaque walls do not propagate anything. By using a policy language based on the metaphor of physical walls, the authors expect that users will find this abstraction to be an intuitive way to control access to their digital footprints.

4.3.1.3 Multiple Faces

Users predefine a small set of disclosure policies, thinking of each one as a different public "face" they might wear [56]. This technique simplifies the definition of multiple permutations of privacy preferences using the metaphor of faces to represent different behaviors during the course of a user's everyday life. As the user encounters a new situation, he assumes the appropriate face (e.g., secure shopper, cocktail party, hanging out with friends, anonymous, family outings, traveling abroad, etc.). Users can concern themselves primarily with their collection of faces and less so with the underlying preferences they abstract.

4.3.1.4 Reciprocity

The strongest advantage of this technique is its simplicity [72]—user A reveals as much of himself to user B as user B reveals to user A. In spite of its simplicity, it can be surprisingly effective because it mimics a common (most of the times unconsciously) behavior in the real world when dealing with privacy issues. In fact, it has been shown in several studies that reciprocity is the basis for building trust between two partners [78]. However, it is not easy to implement a completely fair reciprocal system. For example, in the instant messaging XMPP protocol [79], you are allowed to see if a user is online *only* if that user also can see that you are online. However, if a user is much more active than the other one, the relation is no longer reciprocal. Another example is the NESSIE system [67], which claims to be using this technique by disclosing the users who have registered interest to the user producing events—"when you see me I see you." Again, this may not be considered reciprocity—knowing that someone is watching the other does not imply that the latter can see his actions. In fact, it would be more appropriate to consider it as a form of *lookup notification.*

4.3.2 Data Perturbation

Data perturbation is the most effective technique for community context-aware applications whose primary purpose is gathering statistical information. The idea is to perturb a user's sequence of data values such that (i) the individual data items and their trend (i.e., their changes with time) cannot be estimated without large error, while (ii) the distribution of community data at any point in time as well as the average community data trend can be estimated with high accuracy [41]. There are several approaches as follows (see Fig. 4.1): add noise, encryption, chunk replacement, and blurring.

4.3.2.1 Add Noise

This technique perturbs data by adding noise (useless data) before sending it to the server. This must be done in such a way that it prevents an attacker from breaching the privacy of single users while, at the same time, aggregated statistical data is still meaningful and correct. One option to implement this technique is to add random noise drawn independently either from a known distribution [2] or from a rotation scheme [61], after which a reconstruction algorithm is used to estimate the distribution of the original data. However, randomness may not necessarily imply uncertainty. It has been repeatedly shown that adding random noise to data does not protect privacy [53]. It is generally easy to reconstruct data from noisy measurements, unless noise is so large that utility cannot be attained from sharing the noisy data. Ganti [41] tries to overcome this problem by using well-known models from which it derives random data. For example, for a traffic reporting application, a model of vehicular traffic can be used to generate the noise distribution. Since the noise is very similar to the data itself, it is much harder to reconstruct personal data, thus defeating privacy attacks.

4.3.2.2 Encryption

This technique works by encrypting all personal context information (e.g., with a symmetric key) transmitted through a secure channel to everyone that is allowed to consume the information [70]. To proof that personal information was indeed produced by a given person, information may be digitally signed (e.g., using a private asymmetrical key). Symmetric cryptography inherits all the traditional shortcomings associated to the use of symmetric key encryption: (i) it is hard to establish a secure channel to transmit the keys; (ii) compromising just one of the consuming devices automatically compromises all the personal information of every person who allowed it to consume their information (since their symmetric keys are stored in the device); and (iii) revoking access to someone implies issuing a new symmetric key and retransmitting it to everyone. Encrypting personal context using asymmetrical cryptography would solve some of those problems but would create others. In particular, it would pose scalability problems since personal information would have to be encrypted with the public key of every consumer (unlike symmetric cryptography, where you only need to encrypt once irrespective of the number of consumers). If the discloser is willing to share information with a large number of consumers and/or produces a steady stream of events, the continuous encryption would put a high burden on the system, with a negative impact on its performance especially on resource-constrained devices such as mobile phones.

4.3.2.3 Chunk Replacement

Mun[60] proposes to replace chunks of data with synthetic but realistic samples that have a limited impact on the quality of the aggregated analysis. Replacing data is a reasonable alternative to *selective hiding* approaches that are prone to raising suspicion and thus losing credibility [55]. For example, if someone is continuously transmitting his location and then suddenly stops, this can lead others to think that person entered a sensitive location (e.g., his home). Mun solves this problem by replacing chunks instead of hiding them. For example, this technique could be used to replace a location trace segment with another closely related to the original in terms of model output equivalency, based on historical information of the user's likely movements. To be effective and believable, the substitute trace must be credible to the people with whom the user shares his data.

4.3.2.4 Blurring

Blurring refers to disclosing something true but not specific enough to reveal sensitive information and it is a well-known human behavior to control privacy [48]. For example, this happens when someone answers a question with "vague" or "not specific" information to protect his privacy. However, some studies with context-aware applications show that blurring is not commonly used by users, who prefer not to disclose any information instead of blurring it [28]. Still, it is a valid technique derived from the already mentioned "plausible deniability" property.

4.3.3 Anonymization

Anonymization consists of concealing the real identity of the person associated with some context information. To properly evaluate the effectiveness of an anonymization technique we need an objective metric of a person's anonymity. The most well-known metric is *k-anonymity* [92]. It is based on the idea of generalizing a data record until it is indistinguishable from the records of at least $k - 1$ other individuals. This algorithm applied to location information can be implemented with the following steps [43]: location information is represented by a tuple containing three intervals $([x1, x2], [y1, y2], [t1, t2])$. The intervals $[x1, x2]$ and $[y1, y2]$ describe a two-dimensional area where the subject is located. $[t1, t2]$ describes a time period during which the subject was present in the area. Thus, a location tuple for a subject is *k-anonymous*, when it describes not only the location of the subject but also the locations of $k - 1$ other subjects. In other words, $k - 1$ other subjects also must have been present in the area during the time period described by the tuple. Generally speaking, the larger the anonymity set k is, the higher the degree of anonymity is.

The techniques for anonymizing context information usually work by either (see Fig. 4.1) (i) providing a complex multi-hop path between the discloser and the consumer of the information, (ii) replacing the real identity with an incomplete or fake one, or (iii) mixing information from multiple related people.

4.3.3.1 Mix Routing

Originally proposed by [21] to guarantee the anonymity of participants in a electronic mail system, it has since then been applied to various context-aware systems (e.g., AnonySense[29], Mist [3]). A mix is a message router that forwards messages in such a way that an adversary cannot match incoming messages to outgoing messages. This is accomplished by numerous techniques such as padding all messages to the same size, encrypting incoming and outcoming messages with different keys, or reordering messages. Obviously, this technique implies that an adequate network infrastructure is in place, with multiple nodes between the sender and the receiver, which may not be practical in many applications.

4.3.3.2 Pseudonyms

Anonymity concerns the dissociation of information about an individual, such as location, from that individual's actual identity. A special type of anonymity is pseudonyms, where an individual is anonymous, but maintains a persistent identity (a pseudonym) [35]. To reduce the chance of a privacy attack based on the victim's history, Beresford [10] proposes frequently changing pseudonyms.

4.3.3.3 Hitchhiking

Proposed by Tang [93], this algorithm is suitable for applications that use location data collected from multiple people to infer statistical information about a given place, such as the number of seats available in a coffee shop or the number of cars in a bridge. The key idea is that a person does not send his location but rather information that he collected at a given location. For example, in a coffee shop, an application installed in the user's computer continuously scans the WiFi network to determine how many other computers are present. At regular intervals, it reports this count to the server.

4.3.3.4   Spatial-Temporal Cloaking

Gruteser [43] proposes an implementation of k-anonymity based on two variables: location and time. Starting with location, it subdivides the area around the subject's position until the number of subjects in the area falls below a certain threshold k (thus achieving k-anonymity), using quad-tree algorithms. This is called spatial cloaking, because it reduces spatial accuracy. It is also possible to maintain spatial accuracy at the expense of reducing temporal accuracy, by delaying the information availability until k subjects have been in a certain area. By combining both dimensions, it is possible to achieve a high level of anonymity without a big loss of precision. However, it is not suitable to situations where accuracy and timeliness are important.

4.3.3.5   Attribute-Based Authentication

Some applications associate data with some non-identifiable attributes of the user (e.g., age, gender) instead of the user himself, thus guaranteeing anonymity [52]. For example, Alice might reveal that she is a "student at Dartmouth" without disclosing her identity.

4.3.4   Lookup Notification

Lookup notification provides awareness of potential privacy breaches by showing who consumed or is consuming context information of a given person. Since it acts *a posteriori* (after a privacy breach) it is usually used to complement the other three types of techniques, detecting misconfigurations or just giving users more confidence with their privacy settings. There are basically two approaches (see Fig. 4.1): alerts and logs.

4.3.4.1   Alerts

Applications using this technique provide the discloser of information with immediate visual or audio feedback when someone is consuming that information [28]. For example, consider a mobile phone social application which shows an alert message every time a friend queries the owner's location.

4.3.4.2 Logs

Since the abovementioned *alerts* are shown in real time, they can become a source of interruptions leading users to turn them off, defeating its purpose. In that sense, logs represent a less intrusive technique, since they just register all consumptions of personal context information in a log which can be consulted by the information discloser at any time, when he wishes so. On the other hand, if we are in presence of a privacy breach, we will want to reduce the lag between the time of the (undesirable) information consumption and the time of log checking to prevent further private information leakage.

4.4 Summary

This chapter starts with some considerations regarding the definition of privacy in distributed context-aware systems, emphasizing the properties that must be considered: solitude, anonymity, and reservation. In addition, when taking into account a psychological view of the issue, we see that other important properties appear: control, accountability, plausible deniability, reciprocity, and utility. These lead us to propose a taxonomy based on the following main techniques: privacy policies, data perturbation, anonymization, and lookup notification. For each one of these techniques we described the specific solutions that can be found in the literature.

Chapter 5
Conclusions

Abstract This chapter concludes the book by summarizing the main challenges faced by developers of distributed context-aware systems regarding scalability and privacy: (i) efficient and scalable context propagation and (ii) privacy control. The concept of aggregation appears as a result of the inference step, which effectively aggregates raw sensed data into high-level context information, and also appears as an option in push-based systems with delayed updates—since there is a delay, accumulated context data can be aggregated before it is transmitted. Although in different times on the context life cycle, these two types of aggregation achieve the same two important results: reduce the volume of information (an efficient solution to propagation of large volumes of information) and transform information (a practical solution to many privacy problems).

5.1 Scalability

Context information in distributed systems usually flows through four steps: **capture**, **infer**, **distribute**, and **consume**. This division makes the analysis of such systems much easier, because it fits well within typical context-aware architectures and uses simple verbs to denote actions that evolve the state and location of the context information. This book focuses on these actions and tries to answer the question: "what happens to context since it is produced until it is consumed?"

The **capture** step is what triggers the process. Traditionally, context has been captured using physical sensors with the sole objective of providing the user's location. This is changing in two fundamental ways. First, the range of available physical sensors is now much wider, encompassing such devices as accelerometers, thermometers, and photodiodes. Many of these sensors are now bundled with off-the-shelf mobile phones. As more of these sensors are used in the capture step we can expect much larger volumes of sensed data to be distributed to the system components, with the associated risk of network bandwidth exhaustion. Second, as more people use computers on everyday tasks (for work or leisure), the number

P. Ferreira and P. Alves, *Distributed Context-Aware Systems*, SpringerBriefs in Computer Science, DOI 10.1007/978-3-319-04882-6_5, © The Author(s) 2014

of available virtual sensors is also increasing. Time-tracking desktop applications are able to record every user action on a computer. Social network portals such as Facebook or Twitter expose personal status updates, location, and behaviors of millions of users. Face-to-face communication is being replaced by instant messaging, e-mail, and videoconferencing. All these applications are potential virtual sensors and may generate so much information that the problem is no longer the available network bandwidth but rather the user attention bandwidth. The fundamental trade-off in this step is between richer context information and information overload. The sensors at our disposal are more ubiquitous and cheaper than ever, but is the system infrastructure able to cope with all this information?

One possible solution to context information overload lies in the **infer** step. This step is able to transform large volumes of raw sensed data into much smaller high-level information. For example, consider an inference engine that continually transforms megabytes of raw audio data captured from a microphone in a room into a binary representation "occupied" or "empty." However, larger and more complex sensed data requires a more resource-demanding inference engine. Even modern smartphones with last-generation CPUs are not appropriate to run complex inference algorithms which would quickly deplete battery power. As such, this engine is usually deployed in servers with large capacity. Although this solves the performance problem, it creates other problems, such as reduced personalization and increased risk of privacy breach.

The third step deals with context **distribution**. There are three main options to solve this problem, although some systems combine two of them: using a central server (centralized), using multiple central servers, each one responsible for a subset of the system clients (partitioned), and a peer-to-peer approach where each node acts as both server and client. Some distributed context-aware systems present specific requirements that may dictate the distribution approach. For example, such systems usually include mobile components (sensors, mobile phones) that are subject to intermittent connections, which will certainly cause problems on centralized or partitioned architectures. Ironically, most of these systems are centralized, perhaps because the routing algorithm is simpler to implement. Some centralized systems provide an intermediate layer acting as a proxy cache (e.g., UbiqMuseum, GUIDE) that alleviates the problem without actually solving it. Location-aware systems (e.g., BusinessFinder) also imply specific requirements with direct influence in the distribution strategy. A promising approach is to use partitioned architectures, with each server responsible for a geographical region. In fact, depending on the system's goal, any context dimension can be used to partition the client space reducing the probability of multi-hop communications.[1] Peer-to-peer systems are more resilient to intermittent connections and allow greater privacy control but its management is

---

[1]In partitioned systems, multi-hop communication occurs when a client in one partition has to communicate with a client in another partition.

more complex. A possible solution is to combine ad hoc spontaneous peer-to-peer networks between nearby devices with a partitioned or centralized approach (e.g., BikeNet), bringing the advantages of both worlds.

Finally, the **consume** step is directly related to immediacy requirements ("Do client applications need up-to-date context information or do they tolerate some delay?") as well as frequency of updates ("Do sensors continuously produce context events or only sporadically?"). If there are a lot of updates but the client application does not need to receive them right away, a simple pull-based approach is sufficient. For other scenarios, a push-based approach is more efficient, specially if propagation is filtered based on client-defined criteria. For applications that do not require immediate propagation, combining a delayed approach with aggregation can result in a more efficient use of resources, as shown in Alves [6].

As we have shown, the development of distributed context-aware systems faces many challenges. Among them, we would like to stress two problems and a possible roadmap. These are, in our opinion, the most important problems to be solved in large-scale distributed context-aware systems: (i) efficient and scalable context propagation and (ii) privacy control. None of the surveyed systems in this book solves effectively these two problems.

At first sight, they seem to be unrelated problems but a closer look detects a high correlation between them. For example, delegating the inference step into middleware components may increase the system scalability but creates privacy issues, as raw sensed data is no longer under the user's control. Interestingly, we believe there is a technique that may solve both problems: **aggregation**. The term aggregation appears twice in this book to mean slightly different things. First, it appears as a result of the inference step, which effectively aggregates raw sensed data into high-level context information. Second, it appears as an option in push-based systems with delayed updates—since there is a delay, accumulated context data can be aggregated before it is transmitted. Although in different times on the context life cycle, these two types of aggregation achieve the same two important results:

- **Reduce the volume of information**—an efficient solution to propagation of large volumes of information. The more system components apply aggregation, the more scalable the system is.
- **Transform information**—a practical solution to many privacy problems. By judiciously combining or transforming information, we can effectively anonymize personal data.

As an example, consider the aggregation of data from a GPS device continuously tracking our position. By aggregating all this data into high-level sparse context information such as "at work" or "at cinema," we greatly reduce consumption of system resources while, at the same time, protect the user's privacy.

When referring to privacy management techniques, the term aggregation is also used as a means to increase entropy of personal sensitive information, thereby assuring increased privacy protection to the end users. For example, one of the most promising anonymization techniques called spatial-temporal cloaking consists of transmitting someone's location only when there are enough users in the vicinity also transmitting their location. In that case, the location is aggregated into something like "In the last 5 min, there were nine people in Lisbon Cathedral," which still carries important context information without revealing the identity of the people involved.

5.2 Privacy

Privacy management is a complex yet critical issue on distributed context-aware systems. Although there has been extensive research on this subject, with the proposal of multiple techniques as shown on this book, we are still far from reaching a complete solution that covers the privacy properties described by Raento [72], derived from decades of social psychology studies: *control*, *accountability*, *plausible deniability*, *reciprocity*, and *utility*. For example, **privacy policies** give people the power to control who can consume their personal information, but still in a very rigid immutable way, when Consolvo's studies [28] showed that privacy settings are very dynamic and completely situation-dependent. **Data perturbation** techniques are, likewise, applied regardless of the situation—encryption and chunk replacement do not take into account the relation between the discloser and the consumer or other environmental variables.

In fact, the rigidity of most techniques is their bigger shortcoming for wide adoption, since they do not mimic human highly dynamic behaviors when it comes to privacy preservation. Still, some techniques manage to get closer to those behaviors as is the case of techniques that try to achieve **k-anonymity** such as **spatial-temporal cloaking**, whose dynamics are based on the level of entropy that gives the user sufficient confidence on the preservation of his private data. We increase entropy by aggregating related data, it being the real-world example of only allowing video-vigilance on public (typically crowded) places or location-based applications that only transmit their users' location where there are enough users in the vicinity also transmitting their location. Another advantage of techniques that dynamically increase entropy is their implicit support for **plausible deniability**, since the interpretation gaps that arise from (incomplete) aggregated information are left to the discloser to fill in with the most appropriate information within the current situation.

In addition, although **lookup notification** cannot avoid privacy breaches (since they act a posteriori), it should not be dismissed as a valid privacy management technique, since it gives user confidence that the other mechanisms in place are in fact protecting their privacy.

Finally, it is noteworthy that highly successful commercial applications such as Facebook and Twitter are aware of the privacy issues that can arise from misuse of their systems but still provide very limited privacy management mechanisms resorting only to cumbersome and error-prone checklists, which are a complete departure from deeply rooted human behaviors, as formed and refined during decades of social adaptation.

References

1. Abowd, G.D., Dey, A.K., Brown, P.J., Davies, N., Smith, M., Steggles, P.: Towards a better understanding of context and context awareness. In: Proceedings of the 1st International Symposium on Handheld and Ubiquitous Computing, HUC '99, pp. 304–307. Springer, London (1999). http://dl.acm.org/citation.cfm?id=647985.743843
2. Agrawal, R., Srikant, R.: Privacy-preserving data mining. SIGMOD Rec. **29**(2), 439–450 (2000). doi:10.1145/335191.335438. http://doi.acm.org/10.1145/335191.335438
3. Al-Muhtadi, J., Campbell, R., Kapadia, A., Mickunas, M., Yi, S.: Routing through the mist: privacy preserving communication in ubiquitous computing environments. In: Proceedings of 22nd International Conference on Distributed Computing Systems 2002, pp. 74–83 (2002). doi:10.1109/ICDCS.2002.1022244
4. Allavena, A., Demers, A., Hopcroft, J.E.: Correctness of a gossip based membership protocol. In: Proceedings of the 24th Annual ACM Symposium on Principles of Distributed Computing, PODC '05, pp. 292–301. ACM, New York (2005). doi:10.1145/1073814.1073871. http://doi.acm.org/10.1145/1073814.1073871
5. Altman, I., Vinsel, A., Brown, B.: Dialectic conceptions in social psychology: an application to social penetration and privacy regulation. Adv. Exp. Soc. Psychol. **14**, 107–160 (1981)
6. Alves, P., Ferreira, P.: Reconmuc: adaptable consistency requirements for efficient large-scale multi-user chat. In: Proceedings of the ACM 2011 Conference on Computer Supported Cooperative Work, CSCW '11, pp. 553–562. ACM, New York (2011). doi:10.1145/1958824.1958909. http://doi.acm.org/10.1145/1958824.1958909
7. Baldauf, M., Dustdar, S., Rosenberg, F.: A survey on context- aware systems. Int. J. Ad Hoc Ubiquitous Comput. **2**(4), 263–277 (2007). doi:10.1504/IJAHUC.2007.014070. http://dx.doi.org/10.1504/IJAHUC.2007.014070
8. Bardram, J.E., Hansen, T.R.: The aware architecture: supporting context-mediated social awareness in mobile cooperation. In: Proceedings of the 2004 ACM Conference on Computer Supported Cooperative Work, CSCW '04, pp. 192–201. ACM, New York (2004). doi:10.1145/1031607.1031639. http://doi.acm.org/10.1145/1031607.1031639
9. Bardram, J.E., Hansen, T.R., Soegaard, M.: Awaremedia: a shared interactive display supporting social, temporal, and spatial awareness in surgery. In: Proceedings of the 2006 20th Anniversary Conference on Computer Supported Cooperative Work, CSCW '06, pp. 109–118. ACM, New York (2006). doi:10.1145/1180875.1180892. http://doi.acm.org/10.1145/1180875.1180892
10. Beresford, A., Stajano, F.: Location privacy in pervasive computing. IEEE Pervasive Comput. **2**(1), 46–55 (2003). doi:10.1109/MPRV.2003.1186725

11. Bjerrum, E., Bødker, S.: Learning and living in the 'new office'. In: Kuutti, K., Karsten, E., Fitzpatrick, G., Dourish, P., Schmidt, K. (eds.) ECSCW 2003, pp. 199–218. Springer, Netherlands (2003). doi:10.1007/978-94-010-0068-0_11. http://dx.doi.org/10.1007/978-94-010-0068-0_11

12. Bolchini, C., Curino, C.A., Quintarelli, E., Schreiber, F.A., Tanca, L.: A data-oriented survey of context models. SIGMOD Rec. **36**(4), 19–26 (2007). doi:10.1145/1361348.1361353. http://doi.acm.org/10.1145/1361348.1361353

13. Bratskas, P., Paspallis, N., Papadopoulos, G.: An evaluation of the state of the art in context-aware architectures. In: The 16th International Conference on Information Systems Development (ISD 2007). Springer, Heidelberg (2007)

14. Brown, P., Bovey, J., Chen, X.: Context-aware applications: from the laboratory to the marketplace. IEEE Pers. Comm. **4**(5), 58–64 (1997). doi:10.1109/98.626984

15. Cano, J.C., Manzoni, P., Toh, C.K.: Ubiqmuseum: a bluetooth and java based context-aware system for ubiquitous computing. Wireless Pers. Comm. **38**(2), 187–202 (2006). doi:10.1007/s11277-005-9001-x. http://dx.doi.org/10.1007/s11277-005-9001-x

16. Carzaniga, A., Rosenblum, D.S., Wolf, A.L.: Design and evaluation of a wide-area event notification service. ACM Trans. Comput. Syst. **19**(3), 332–383 (2001). doi:10.1145/380749.380767. http://doi.acm.org/10.1145/380749.380767

17. Castro, M., Druschel, P., Kermarrec, A.M., Rowstron, A.I.T.: Scribe: a large-scale and decentralized application-level multicast infrastructure. IEEE J. Sel. Area Comm. **20**(8), 1489–1499 (2002). doi:10.1109/JSAC.2002.803069

18. Castro, M., Jones, M., Kermarrec, A.M., Rowstron, A., Theimer, M., Wang, H., Wolman, A.: An evaluation of scalable application-level multicast built using peer-to-peer overlays. In: The 22nd Annual Joint Conference of the IEEE Computer and Communications, INFOCOM 2003, vol. 2, pp. 1510–1520. IEEE Societies, San Francisco (2003). doi:10.1109/INFCOM.2003.1208986

19. Chakraborty, D., Dasgupta, K., Misra, A.: Efficient querying and resource management using distributed presence information in converged networks. In: Proceedings of the 7th International Conference on Mobile Data Management, MDM '06, p. 28. IEEE Computer Society, Washington (2006). doi:10.1109/MDM.2006.81. http://dx.doi.org/10.1109/MDM.2006.81

20. Chakraborty, D., Dasgupta, K., Mittal, S., Misra, A., Gupta, A., Newmark, E., Oberle, C.: Businessfinder: harnessing presence to enable live yellow pages for small, medium and micro mobile businesses. IEEE Comm. Mag. **45**(1), 144–151 (2007). doi:10.1109/MCOM.2007.284550

21. Chaum, D.L.: Untraceable electronic mail, return addresses, and digital pseudonyms. Comm. ACM **24**(2), 84–90 (1981). doi:10.1145/358549.358563. http://doi.acm.org/10.1145/358549.358563

22. Chen, G., Kotz, D.: A survey of context-aware mobile computing research. Dartmouth Computer Science Technical Report TR2000-381, pp. 1–16 (2000)

23. Chen, G., Kotz, D.: Context aggregation and dissemination in ubiquitous computing systems. In: Proceedings of the 4th IEEE Workshop on Mobile Computing Systems and Applications, WMCSA '02, pp. 105–14. IEEE Computer Society, Washington (2002). http://dl.acm.org/citation.cfm?id=832315.837559

24. Chen, G., Li, M., Kotz, D.: Design and implementation of a large-scale context fusion network. In: Mobile and Ubiquitous Systems: Networking and Services, 2004. The 1st Annual International Conference on MOBIQUITOUS 2004, pp. 246–255 (2004). doi:10.1109/MOBIQ.2004.1331731

25. Cheverst, K., Mitchell, K., Davies, N.: Design of an object model for a context sensitive tourist {GUIDE}. Comput. Graph. **23**(6), 883–891 (1999). doi:http://dx.doi.org/10.1016/S0097-8493(99)00119-3. http://www.sciencedirect.com/science/article/pii/S0097849399001193

26. Cheverst, K., Smith, G., Mitchell, K., Friday, A., Davies, N.: The role of shared context in supporting cooperation between city visitors. Comput. Graph. **25**(4), 555–562 (2001). doi:http://dx.doi.org/10.1016/S0097-8493(01)00083-8. http://www.sciencedirect.com/science/article/pii/S0097849301000838.
27. Cheverst, K., Mitchell, K., Davies, N.: Exploring context-aware information push. Pers. Ubiquit. Comput. **6**(4), 276–281 (2002). doi:10.1007/s007790200028. http://dx.doi.org/10.1007/s007790200028
28. Consolvo, S., Smith, I.E., Matthews, T., LaMarca, A., Tabert, J., Powledge, P.: Location disclosure to social relations: why, when, and what people want to share. In: Proceedings of the SIGCHI Conference on Human Factors in Computing Systems, CHI '05, pp. 81–90. ACM, New York (2005). doi:10.1145/1054972.1054985. http://doi.acm.org/10.1145/1054972.1054985
29. Cornelius, C., Kapadia, A., Kotz, D., Peebles, D., Shin, M., Triandopoulos, N.: Anonysense: privacy-aware people-centric sensing. In: Proceedings of the 6th International Conference on Mobile systems, Applications, and Services, MobiSys '08, pp. 211–224. ACM, New York (2008). doi:10.1145/1378600.1378624. http://doi.acm.org/10.1145/1378600.1378624
30. Cornwell, J., Fette, I., Hsieh, G., Prabaker, M., Rao, J., Tang, K., Vaniea, K., Bauer, L., Cranor, L., Hong, J., McLaren, B., Reiter, M., Sadeh, N.: User-controllable security and privacy for pervasive computing. In: Mobile Computing Systems and Applications, 2007. The 8th IEEE Workshop on HotMobile 2007, pp. 14–19 (2007). doi:10.1109/HotMobile.2007.9
31. Cowzer, N., Quigley, A.: Geoigm: a location-aware igm platform. In: Enabling Technologies: Infrastructures for Collaborative Enterprises, 2009. The 18th IEEE International Workshops on WETICE '09, pp. 105–110 (2009). doi:10.1109/WETICE.2009.29
32. Demers, A., Greene, D., Houser, C., Irish, W., Larson, J., Shenker, S., Sturgis, H., Swinehart, D., Terry, D.: Epidemic algorithms for replicated database maintenance. SIGOPS Oper. Syst. Rev. **22**(1), 8–32 (1988). doi:10.1145/43921.43922. http://doi.acm.org/10.1145/43921.43922
33. Dey, A., Mankoff, J., Abowd, G., Carter, S.: Distributed mediation of ambiguous context in aware environments. In: Proceedings of the 15th Annual ACM Symposium on User Interface Software and Technology, UIST '02, pp. 121–130. ACM, New York (2002). doi:10.1145/571985.572003. http://doi.acm.org/10.1145/571985.572003
34. Dourish, P., Bellotti, V.: Awareness and coordination in shared workspaces. In: Proceedings of the 1992 ACM Conference on Computer-Supported Cooperative Work, CSCW '92, pp. 107–114. ACM, New York (1992). doi:10.1145/143457.143468. http://doi.acm.org/10.1145/143457.143468
35. Duckham, M., Kulik, L.: Location privacy and location-aware computing. In: Dynamic and Mobile GIS: Investigating Change in Space and Time, pp. 34–51. CRC Press, Boca Raton (2006)
36. Eisenman, S.B., Miluzzo, E., Lane, N.D., Peterson, R.A., Ahn, G.S., Campbell, A.T.: The bikenet mobile sensing system for cyclist experience mapping. In: Proceedings of the 5th International Conference on Embedded Networked Sensor Systems, SenSys '07, pp. 87–101. ACM, New York (2007). doi:10.1145/1322263.1322273. http://doi.acm.org/10.1145/1322263.1322273
37. Eugster, P.T., Felber, P.A., Guerraoui, R., Kermarrec, A.M.: The many faces of publish/subscribe. ACM Comput. Surv. **35**(2), 114–131 (2003). doi:10.1145/857076.857078. http://doi.acm.org/10.1145/857076.857078
38. Fitzpatrick, G., Mansfield, T., Kaplan, S., Arnold, D., Phelps, T., Segall, B.: Augmenting the workaday world with elvin. In: Bødker, S., Kyng, M., Schmidt, K. (eds.) ECSCW '99, pp. 431–450. Springer, Netherlands (2002). doi:10.1007/0-306-47316-X_23. http://dx.doi.org/10.1007/0-306-47316-X_23
39. Fogarty, J., Hudson, S.E.: Toolkit support for developing and deploying sensor-based statistical models of human situations. In: Proceedings of the SIGCHI Conference on Human Factors in Computing Systems, CHI '07, pp. 135–144. ACM, New York (2007). doi:10.1145/1240624.1240645. http://doi.acm.org/10.1145/1240624.1240645

40. Fogarty, J., Lai, J., Christensen, J.: Presence versus availability: the design and evaluation of a context-aware communication client. Int. J. Hum. Comput. Stud. **61**(3), 299–317 (2004). doi:http://dx.doi.org/10.1016/j.ijhcs.2003.12.016. http://www.sciencedirect.com/science/article/pii/S1071581903002222

41. Ganti, R.K., Pham, N., Tsai, Y.E., Abdelzaher, T.F.: Poolview: stream privacy for grassroots participatory sensing. In: Proceedings of the 6th ACM Conference on Embedded Network Sensor Systems, SenSys '08, pp. 281–294. ACM, New York (2008). doi:10.1145/1460412.1460440. http://doi.acm.org/10.1145/1460412.1460440

42. Gross, R., Acquisti, A.: Information revelation and privacy in online social networks. In: Proceedings of the 2005 ACM Workshop on Privacy in the Electronic Society, WPES '05, pp. 71–80. ACM, New York (2005). doi:10.1145/1102199.1102214. http://doi.acm.org/10.1145/1102199.1102214

43. Gruteser, M., Grunwald, D.: Anonymous usage of location-based services through spatial and temporal cloaking. In: Proceedings of the 1st International Conference on Mobile Systems, Applications and Services, MobiSys '03, pp. 31–42. ACM, New York (2003). doi:10.1145/1066116.1189037. http://doi.acm.org/10.1145/1066116.1189037

44. Gutwin, C., Schneider, K., Paquette, D., Penner, R.: Supporting group awareness in distributed software development. In: Bastide, R., Palanque, P., Roth, J. (eds.) Engineering Human Computer Interaction and Interactive Systems. Lecture Notes in Computer Science, vol. 3425, pp. 383–397. Springer, Berlin (2005). doi:10.1007/11431879_25. http://dx.doi.org/10.1007/11431879_25

45. Henricksen, K., Indulska, J., McFadden, T., Balasubramaniam, S.: Middleware for distributed context-aware systems. In: Meersman, R., Tari, Z. (eds.) On the Move to Meaningful Internet Systems 2005: CoopIS, DOA, and ODBASE. Lecture Notes in Computer Science, vol. 3760, pp. 846–863. Springer, Berlin (2005). doi:10.1007/11575771_53. http://dx.doi.org/10.1007/11575771_53

46. Hightower, J., Borriello, G.: Location systems for ubiquitous computing. Computer **34**(8), 57–66 (2001). doi:10.1109/2.940014. http://dx.doi.org/10.1109/2.940014

47. Hofer, T., Schwinger, W., Pichler, M., Leonhartsberger, G., Altmann, J., Retschitzegger, W.: Context-awareness on mobile devices: the hydrogen approach. In: Proceedings of the 36th Annual Hawaii International Conference on System Sciences 2003, p. 10 (2003) doi:10.1109/HICSS.2003.1174831

48. Iachello, G., Smith, I., Consolvo, S., Chen, M., Abowd, G.D.: Developing privacy guidelines for social location disclosure applications and services. In: Proceedings of the 2005 Symposium on Usable Privacy and Security, SOUPS '05, pp. 65–76. ACM, New York (2005). doi:10.1145/1073001.1073008. http://doi.acm.org/10.1145/1073001.1073008

49. Indulska, J., Sutton, P.: Location management in pervasive systems. In: Proceedings of the Australasian Information Security Workshop Conference on ACSW Frontiers 2003, vol. 21, pp. 143–151. Australian Computer Society, Inc., Darlinghurst (2003). http://dl.acm.org/citation.cfm?id=827987.828003

50. Jovanovic, M.: Modeling large-scale peer-to-peer networks and a case study of Gnutella. Ph.D. thesis, University of Cincinnati (2001). http://etd.ohiolink.edu/view.cgi?ucin989967592

51. Kapadia, A., Henderson, T., Fielding, J., Kotz, D.: Virtual walls: Protecting digital privacy in pervasive environments. In: LaMarca, A., Langheinrich, M., Truong, K. (eds.) Pervasive Computing. Lecture Notes in Computer Science, vol. 4480, pp. 162–179. Springer, Berlin (2007). doi:10.1007/978-3-540-72037-9_10. http://dx.doi.org/10.1007/978-3-540-72037-9_10

52. Kapadia, A., Kotz, D., Triandopoulos, N.: Opportunistic sensing: Security challenges for the new paradigm. In: The 1st International Conference on Communication Systems and Networks and Workshops COMSNETS 2009, pp. 1–10 (2009). doi:10.1109/COMSNETS.2009.4808850

53. Kargupta, H., Datta, S., Wang, Q., Sivakumar, K.: On the privacy preserving properties of random data perturbation techniques. In: Third IEEE International Conference on Data Mining 2003 (ICDM 2003), pp. 99–106 (2003). doi:10.1109/ICDM.2003.1250908

54. Laerhoven, K.: Combining the self-organizing map and k-means clustering for on-line classification of sensor data. In: Dorffner, G., Bischof, H., Hornik, K. (eds.) Artificial Neural Networks - ICANN 2001. Lecture Notes in Computer Science, vol. 2130, pp. 464–469. Springer, Berlin (2001). doi:10.1007/3-540-44668-0_65. http://dx.doi.org/10.1007/3-540-44668-0_65

55. Lane, N., Miluzzo, E., Lu, H., Peebles, D., Choudhury, T., Campbell, A.: A survey of mobile phone sensing. IEEE Comm. Mag. **48**(9), 140–150 (2010). doi:10.1109/MCOM.2010.5560598

56. Lederer, S., Dey, A.K., Mankoff, J.: A conceptual model and a metaphor of everyday privacy in ubiquitous. Technical Report. University of California at Berkeley, Berkeley (2002)

57. Lu, H., Pan, W., Lane, N.D., Choudhury, T., Campbell, A.T.: Soundsense: scalable sound sensing for people-centric applications on mobile phones. In: Proceedings of the 7th International Conference on Mobile Systems, Applications, and Services, MobiSys '09, pp. 165–178. ACM, New York (2009). doi:10.1145/1555816.1555834. http://doi.acm.org/10.1145/1555816.1555834

58. Mathur, A.G., Hall, R.W., Jahanian, F., Prakash, A., Rasmussen, C.: The Publish/Subscribe Paradigm for Scalable Group Collaboration Systems. Technical Report CSE-TR-270-95. Department of Electrical Engineering and Computer Science, University of Michigan, Ann Arbor (1995)

59. Miluzzo, E., Lane, N.D., Fodor, K., Peterson, R., Lu, H., Musolesi, M., Eisenman, S.B., Zheng, X., Campbell, A.T.: Sensing meets mobile social networks: the design, implementation and evaluation of the cenceme application. In: Proceedings of the 6th ACM Conference on Embedded Network Sensor Systems, SenSys '08, pp. 337–350. ACM, New York (2008). doi:10.1145/1460412.1460445. http://doi.acm.org/10.1145/1460412.1460445

60. Mun, M., Reddy, S., Shilton, K., Yau, N., Burke, J., Estrin, D., Hansen, M., Howard, E., West, R., Boda, P.: Peir, the personal environmental impact report, as a platform for participatory sensing systems research. In: Proceedings of the 7th International Conference on Mobile Systems, Applications, and Services, MobiSys '09, pp. 55–68. ACM, New York (2009). doi:10.1145/1555816.1555823. http://doi.acm.org/10.1145/1555816.1555823

61. Oliveira, S., Zaïane, O.: Achieving privacy preservation when sharing data for clustering. In: Jonker, W., Petkovic, M. (eds.) Secure Data Management. Lecture Notes in Computer Science, vol. 3178, pp. 67–82. Springer, Berlin (2004). doi:10.1007/978-3-540-30073-1_6. http://dx.doi.org/10.1007/978-3-540-30073-1_6

62. Oulasvirta, A., Raento, M., Tiitta, S.: Contextcontacts: re-designing smartphone's contact book to support mobile awareness and collaboration. In: Proceedings of the 7th International Conference on Human Computer Interaction with Mobile Devices and Services, MobileHCI '05, pp. 167–174. ACM, New York (2005). doi:10.1145/1085777.1085805. http://doi.acm.org/10.1145/1085777.1085805

63. Oyomno, W., Jäppinen, P., Kerttula, E.: Privacy implications of context-aware services. In: Proceedings of the 4th International ICST Conference on Communication System Software and Middleware, COMSWARE '09, pp. 17:1–17:9. ACM, New York (2009). doi:10.1145/1621890.1621913. http://doi.acm.org/10.1145/1621890.1621913

64. Pascoe, J., Ryan, N., Morse, D.: Human-computer-giraffe interaction: HCI in the field. Technology (1998). http://kar.kent.ac.uk/21665/

65. Plale, B., Liu, Y.: Survey of publish subscribe event systems. Technical Report TR574, Indiana University (2003)

66. Prekop, P., Burnett, M.: Activities, context and ubiquitous computing. Comput. Comm. **26**(11), 1168–1176 (2003). doi:http://dx.doi.org/10.1016/S0140-3664(02)00251-7. http://www.sciencedirect.com/science/article/pii/S0140366402002517.

67. Prinz, W.: Nessie: an awareness environment for cooperative settings. In: Bødker, S., Kyng, M., Schmidt, K. (eds.) ECSCW '99, pp. 391–410. Springer, Netherlands (2002). doi:10.1007/0-306-47316-X_21. http://dx.doi.org/10.1007/0-306-47316-X_21

68. Priyantha, N.B., Chakraborty, A., Balakrishnan, H.: The cricket location-support system. In: Proceedings of the 6th Annual International Conference on Mobile Computing and Networking, MobiCom '00, pp. 32–43. ACM, New York (2000). doi:10.1145/345910.345917. http://doi.acm.org/10.1145/345910.345917

69. Priyantha, B., Lymberopoulos, D., Liu, J.: Littlerock: enabling energy-efficient continuous sensing on mobile phones. IEEE Pervasive Comput. 10(2), 12–15 (2011). doi:10.1109/MPRV.2011.28

70. Puttaswamy, K.P.N., Zhao, B.Y.: Preserving privacy in location-based mobile social applications. In: Proceedings of the 11th Workshop on Mobile Computing Systems & Applications, HotMobile '10, pp. 1–6. ACM, New York (2010). doi:10.1145/1734583.1734585. http://doi.acm.org/10.1145/1734583.1734585

71. Quinlan, J.: Induction of decision trees. Mach. Learn. 1(1), 81–106 (1986). doi:10.1007/BF00116251. http://dx.doi.org/10.1007/BF00116251

72. Raento, M., Oulasvirta, A., Petit, R., Toivonen, H.: Contextphone: a prototyping platform for context-aware mobile applications. IEEE Pervasive Comput. 4(2), 51–59 (2005). doi:10.1109/MPRV.2005.29

73. Rana, R.K., Chou, C.T., Kanhere, S.S., Bulusu, N., Hu, W.: Ear-phone: an end-to-end participatory urban noise mapping system. In: Proceedings of the 9th ACM/IEEE International Conference on Information Processing in Sensor Networks, IPSN '10, pp. 105–116. ACM, New York (2010). doi:10.1145/1791212.1791226. http://doi.acm.org/10.1145/1791212.1791226

74. Randell, C., Muller, H.: Context awareness by analysing accelerometer data. In: The 4th International Symposium on Wearable Computers, pp. 175–176 (2000). doi:10.1109/ISWC.2000.888488

75. Ratnasamy, S., Karp, B., Yin, L., Yu, F., Estrin, D., Govindan, R., Shenker, S.: Ght: a geographic hash table for data-centric storage. In: Proceedings of the 1st ACM International Workshop on Wireless Sensor Networks and Applications, WSNA '02, pp. 78–87. ACM, New York (2002). doi:10.1145/570738.570750. http://doi.acm.org/10.1145/570738.570750

76. Reddy, S., Parker, A., Hyman, J., Burke, J., Estrin, D., Hansen, M.: Image browsing, processing, and clustering for participatory sensing: lessons from a dietsense prototype. In: Proceedings of the 4th Workshop on Embedded Networked Sensors, pp. 13–17. ACM, New York (2007). http://portal.acm.org/citation.cfm?id=1278975

77. Riché, S., Brebner, G.: Storing and accessing user context. In: Chen, M.S., Chrysanthis, P., Sloman, M., Zaslavsky, A. (eds.) Mobile Data Management. Lecture Notes in Computer Science, vol. 2574, pp. 1–12. Springer, Berlin (2003). doi:10.1007/3-540-36389-0_1. http://dx.doi.org/10.1007/3-540-36389-0_1

78. Rubin, Z.: Disclosing oneself to a stranger: Reciprocity and its limits. J. Exp. Soc. Psychol. 11(3), 233–260 (1975). doi:http://dx.doi.org/10.1016/S0022-1031(75)80025-4. http://www.sciencedirect.com/science/article/pii/S0022103175800254

79. Saint-Andre, P.: Streaming xml with jabber/xmpp. IEEE Internet Comput. 9(5), 82–89 (2005). doi:10.1109/MIC.2005.110

80. Saito, Y., Shapiro, M.: Optimistic replication. ACM Comput. Surv. 37(1), 42–81 (2005). doi:10.1145/1057977.1057980. http://doi.acm.org/10.1145/1057977.1057980

81. Salber, D., Dey, A.K., Abowd, G.D.: The context toolkit: aiding the development of context-enabled applications. In: Proceedings of the SIGCHI Conference on Human Factors in Computing Systems, CHI '99, pp. 434–441. ACM, New York (1999). doi:10.1145/302979.303126. http://doi.acm.org/10.1145/302979.303126

82. Santos, A., Tarrataca, L., Cardoso, J., Ferreira, D., Diniz, P., Chainho, P.: Context inference for mobile applications in the upcase project. In: Bonnin, J.M., Giannelli, C., Magedanz, T. (eds.) Mobile Wireless Middleware, Operating Systems, and Applications. Lecture Notes of the Institute for Computer Sciences, Social Informatics and Telecommunications Engineering, vol. 7, pp. 352–365. Springer, Berlin (2009). doi:10.1007/978-3-642-01802-2_26. http://dx.doi.org/10.1007/978-3-642-01802-2_26

83. Satyanarayanan, M.: Pervasive computing: vision and challenges. IEEE Pers. Comm. **8**(4), 10–17 (2001). doi:10.1109/98.943998
84. Sawyer, S., Guinan, P.: Software development: processes and performance. IBM Syst. J. **37**(4), 552–569 (1998). doi:10.1147/sj.374.0552
85. Schilit, B., Adams, N., Want, R.: Context-aware computing applications. In: Proceedings of the 1st Workshop on Mobile Computing Systems and Applications 1994, WMCSA '94, pp. 85–90. IEEE Computer Society, Washington (1994). doi:10.1109/WMCSA.1994.16. http://dx.doi.org/10.1109/WMCSA.1994.16
86. Schmidt, A., Beigl, M., Gellersen, H.W.: There is more to context than location. Comput. Graph. **23**(6), 893–901 (1999). doi:http://dx.doi.org/10.1016/S0097-8493(99)00120-X. http://www.sciencedirect.com/science/article/pii/S009784939900120X
87. Segall, B., Arnold, D.: Elvin has left the building: a publish/subscribe notification service with quenching. In: Proceedings AVVG 1997, Brisbane (1997)
88. Segall, B., Arnold, D., Boot, J., Henderson, M., Phelps, T.: Content based routing with elvin4. In: Proceedings of AUUG'00 (2000)
89. Shirky, C.: A group is its worst enemy. http://www.shirky.com/writings/group_enemy.html (2003).
90. Simão, J., Ribeiro, C., Ferreira, P., Veiga, L.: Jano: location-privacy enforcement in mobile and pervasive environments through declarative policies. J. Internet Serv. Appl. **3**, 291–310 (2012). doi:10.1007/s13174-012-0065-z. http://dx.doi.org/10.1007/s13174-012-0065-z
91. Stiefmeier, T., Lombriser, C., Roggen, D., Junker, H., Ogris, G., Troester, G.: Event based activity tracking in work environments. In: The 3rd International Forum on Applied Wearable Computing (IFAWC) 2006, pp. 1–10 (2006)
92. Sweeney, L.: k-anonymity: a model for protecting privacy. Int. J. Uncertain. Fuzziness Knowl. Based Syst. **10**(5), 557–570 (2002). doi:10.1142/S0218488502001648. http://dx.doi.org/10.1142/S0218488502001648
93. Tang, K.P., Keyani, P., Fogarty, J., Hong, J.I.: Putting people in their place: an anonymous and privacy-sensitive approach to collecting sensed data in location-based applications. In: Proceedings of the SIGCHI Conference on Human Factors in Computing Systems, CHI '06, pp. 93–102. ACM, New York (2006). doi:10.1145/1124772.1124788. http://doi.acm.org/10.1145/1124772.1124788
94. Van Laerhoven, K., Cakmakci, O.: What shall we teach our pants? In: The 4th International Symposium on Wearable Computers, pp. 77–83 (2000). doi:10.1109/ISWC.2000.888468
95. Wang, F.Y., Carley, K., Zeng, D., Mao, W.: Social computing: from social informatics to social intelligence. IEEE Intell. Syst. **22**(2), 79–83 (2007). doi:10.1109/MIS.2007.41
96. Weiser, M.: The Computer for the 21st Century. Scientific American, New York (1995). http://wiki.daimi.au.dk/pca/_files/weiser-orig.pdf
97. Welbourne, E., Lester, J., LaMarca, A., Borriello, G.: Mobile context inference using low-cost sensors. In: Strang, T., Linnhoff-Popien, C. (eds.) Location- and Context-Awareness. Lecture Notes in Computer Science, vol. 3479, pp. 254–263. Springer, Berlin (2005). doi:10.1007/11426646_24. http://dx.doi.org/10.1007/11426646_24
98. Westin, A.: Privacy and Freedom, vol. 97. Atheneum, New York (1967). http://www.disi.unige.it/person/CaninoD/bibtex/wes67privacy.txt
99. Widrow, B., Rumelhart, D.E., Lehr, M.A.: Neural networks: applications in industry, business and science. Comm. ACM **37**(3), 93–105 (1994). doi:10.1145/175247.175257. http://doi.acm.org/10.1145/175247.175257
100. Zander, S., Schandl, B.: A framework for context-driven rdf data replication on mobile devices. In: Proceedings of the 6th International Conference on Semantic Systems, I-SEMANTICS '10, pp. 22:1–22:5. ACM, New York (2010). doi:10.1145/1839707.1839735. http://doi.acm.org/10.1145/1839707.1839735